A HANDBOOK FOR LEAs
Second Edition

D1784058

Agnes McMahon is a Research Fellow in the School of Education at the University of Bristol. She has acted as consultant and researcher to LEAs, the DES, the Schools Council and the Training Agency and is currently co-ordinating the Teacher Appraisal Pilot Schemes. She has published widely on teacher induction, school self-review, management development and teacher appraisal.

Ray Bolam is Director of the National Development Centre for Educational Management and Policy and of Further Professional Studies in the University of Bristol. He has acted as a consultant and researcher for LEAs, the DES, OECD and for several governments. He has published widely in the field of professional development and the management of educational change.

Management Development and Educational Reform

A HANDBOOK FOR LEAs

Second Edition

AGNES McMAHON
and
RAY BOLAM

P·C·P
Paul Chapman
Publishing Ltd

First published 1990
Paul Chapman Publishing
144 Liverpool Road
London N1 1LA

British Library Cataloguing in Publication Data

McMahon, Agnes
  A handbook for LEA's. – 2nd ed. – (Management development
  and educational reform).
  1. England. Local education authorities. Administration
  I. Title   II. Bolam, Ray   III. Series
  379.1530942

  ISBN 1 85396 082 9

Typeset by Inforum Typesetting, Portsmouth
Printed and bound in Great Britain by
Butler & Tanner Ltd, Frome and London

CONTENTS

FOREWORD AND ACKNOWLEDGEMENTS

There are three books on school management development in this series. They are as follows:

- *Management Development and Educational Reform: A Handbook for LEAs.*
- *Management Development and Educational Reform: A Handbook for Primary Schools.*
- *Management Development and Educational Reform: A Handbook for Secondary Schools.*

The two schools books include material of relevance to middle and special schools.

All three were originally developed in collaboration with advisers, officers, head-teachers and teachers in 53 schools and eight LEAs. We are extremely grateful for the invaluable help and advice received from the LEA co-ordination teams in the eight pilot LEAs, who tried out and then commented on the draft materials, and also supplied many of the illustrative examples: In Birmingham, Ken Lambert, Jean Carter and Arnold Ingoldsby; in Cambridgeshire, Colin Curtis, John Pearce and Charles Dodd; in Cleveland, Harold Heller, Brian Bailey and Ken Oakley; in Dorset, Peter Mann, Peter McGargle and John Farthing; in Gwent, Russell Cooper, Ian Lewis and Jeff Portch; in Leeds, Stuart Johnson Margaret McIntosh, John West and Arthur Harvey; in North-amptonshire, Roger Martin, Dan Dingle, Bill Shaw and George Gyte; and in South Glamorgan, Derrick Orrell, Ivor Evenden and Eddie Roberts.

The original National Development Centre (NDC) booklets have now been substan-tially extended and up-dated to take account of the many changes resulting from the Education Reform Act and related developments. In this re-writing process, we have taken into account the comments of visitors, associates and participants in NDC con-ferences – to all these we express our thanks.

We have also benefited from the ideas and advice of current and former NDC team members and associates: Valerie Hall, David Oldroyd, Harry Powell, Arthur Spencer,

Mike Wallace, Ron Abbott, Jon Bailey, Elizabeth Ballinger, Michael Birchenough, Mike Murphy and Cyril Poster.

Finally, we wish to thank our colleagues in the support staff who have provided enormous help in preparing this book, particularly Joan Moore and June Collins.

1

INTRODUCTION: SCHOOL MANAGEMENT DEVELOPMENT AND EDUCATIONAL REFORM

One of the most significant aspects of educational policy in the 1980s has been the increased emphasis placed on the provision of management training for headteachers and members of their staff. The government has actively promoted this. First, it made available from 1983 to 1986 specific funds for one-term and twenty-day management courses and for the setting up of the National Development Centre (NDC). Second, it has ensured that, since 1987, management development and training has continued to be the top priority for funding under the terms of the Local Education Authority Training Grants Scheme (LEATGS). Third, it has set up the School Management Task Force. The pressure for management training has not all been one way: headteachers and teachers have also made it known to their LEA employers and to their professional associations that they need further training if they are to cope effectively with the increased complexity and growing demands of their work. There is no widespread resistance to school management training; on the contrary, teachers have welcomed opportunities to develop their skills in this area. However, it has rapidly become clear to all concerned that mounting a series of external courses is an unsatisfactory way of improving the managerial skills of the teaching force, and that a broader, longer-term development strategy is required. The challenge facing LEAs and schools is to see if they can put such a strategy into force.

The origins of this book lie in work that the NDC conducted with eight LEAs from 1984 to 1987. The purpose of this work was to explore how LEAs could plan, implement and evaluate an authority-wide management development policy and programme for headteachers and senior staff in schools. The ideas and suggestions generated in this exercise have been refined in subsequent discussions and in work with other authorities. The result is this handbook, which is intended to help senior LEA staff to plan, implement and evaluate a school management development policy and programme that will improve teaching and learning in their authority's schools. It does so by suggesting ways of improving and building upon present practice so that a coherent, policy-led scheme can be developed.

It is aimed at those staff with an LEA-wide responsibility for the development and training of heads and other senior staff in schools. It should be relevant to officers, inspectors and advisers; to teachers' centre leaders; in-service training (INSET) co-ordinators, Technical and Vocational Education Extension (TVEE) co-ordinators; and co-ordinators of Education Support Grant (ESG) schemes. INSET committee members and elected members should also find it useful.

What is School Management Development?

Management development is a subset of staff development: it is, in effect, staff development for those teachers who have school management responsibilities. A more formal working definition – 'management development is the process whereby the management function of an organization is performed with increased effectiveness' – is designed to highlight several important features of management development:

- It is a long-term process, not a series of disconnected activities.
- It consists of more than external courses.
- Its concern is with the overall management function and not simply with the development of individual managers. Hence it embraces, for example, team-building.
- It aims to improve performance and not just to promote individual learning or career development.
- It aims to integrate the needs of the individual manager with those of the organization.
- Its ultimate aim is to improve the quality of teaching and learning.
- It is rooted in the belief that these aims can best be achieved by maximizing the potential of the human resources in the LEA and its schools.

More concretely, management development may be thought of as a generic term that embraces the following three broad components:

1. *Management training* – which refers to short conferences, courses and workshops that emphasize practical information and skills, that do not normally lead to an award or qualification and that may be run by LEAs, schools or by external trainers and consultants from higher education or elsewhere.
2. *Management education* – which refers to secondments and to long, external courses that often emphasize theory and research-based knowledge, and that lead to higher-education and professional qualifications (e.g. specialist school management diplomas and M Eds).
3. *Management support* – which refers to those job-embedded arrangements and procedures for, for example, selection, promotion and career development, appraisal, on-the-job coaching, job rotation, job enhancement, retirement, re-deployment and equal opportunities, which are the responsibility of the LEA and the school.

Whom is School Management Development for?

All teachers have classroom management responsibilities and an increasing majority now have some responsibility for a school management task, and so require management training. However, in the first instance, a management development programme is likely to focus upon heads, deputies, heads of department and other staff with formal school management responsibilities, in other words for achieving the school's goals by working through and with other professional teachers, which are separate and different from their classroom management roles.

Such staff will probably have formal managerial responsibility for one or more of the following key-task areas:

- Strategic planning, including overall policy and aims, and the school's development plan.
- Communication and decision-making structures and roles.
- Curriculum, teaching methods and examinations.
- Staff and staff development.
- Pupils and pupil learning.
- Financial and material resources.
- External relations.
- Monitoring and evaluation of effectiveness.
- Change and development.
- Self-development as a manager.

The 25,000 or so headteachers, and the 30,000 deputy heads, in England and Wales do, of course, have distinctively important school management responsibilities, but there are also at least 70,000 additional staff with a substantial management role and others who need preparation for such roles – and, of course, all teachers contribute to school management to some degree. In an LEA with, say, 350 primary and 60 secondary schools, the main target group for management development will probably be the 410 headteachers, the 500 or so deputy heads and possibly the 600 or so secondary heads of department, etc. In addition, however, LEAs will want to consider the managerial needs of teachers with specialist curriculum roles in primary schools and those middle managers in secondary schools with co-ordination responsibilities, for example, for TVEE and records of achievement. A number of teachers will have management development needs arising from their responsibility for co-ordinating activities (e.g. for INSET or TVEE) in a cluster or consortium of schools.

Educational Reform and the Need for Management Development

It would be difficult to exaggerate the impact of the government's education-policy initiatives on school management and particularly on headteachers and LEAs. All the recent and impending changes have been nationally initiated and all have direct consequences and implications for teachers, pupils and school management. Although many of them resulted from the Education Act 1988, others arising from earlier government initiatives were already in train. The summary timetable in Table 1.1

Table 1.1 Timetable of existing and projected innovations for schools to be introduced by August 1992

Time	Type of school	
	Primary	Secondary
Prior to September 1989	• New conditions of service • Managing INSET, including staff days • New powers for governors • Opportunity to apply for grant-maintained status (schools with over 300 pupils) • Open access to pupil records	• New conditions of service • Managing INSET, including staff days • New powers for governors • Opportunity to apply for grant-maintained status • Open access to records • Technical and Vocational Education Initiative (TVEI) extension • GCSE
September 1989	• All pupils study core and other foundation subjects • Programmes of study, targets and assessment for 5–6-year-olds in mathematics, English and science • Possibly involved in first phase of appraisal • Licensed teachers	• 11–14-year-olds study core and other foundation subjects • Programmes of study, targets and assessment for 11–12-year-olds in mathematics and science • Possibly involved in first phase of appraisal • Licensed teachers
April 1990	• Schools with over 200 pupils possibly involved in first phase of local financial management	• Possibly involved in first phase of local financial management
September 1990	• Programmes of study, etc., for 6–7-year-olds in mathematics, English, science • Programmes of study, etc., for 7–8-year-olds in mathematics, English, science and, possibly, technology	• Programmes of study, etc., for 12–13-year-olds in mathematics and science • Programmes of study, etc., for 11–12-year-olds in English and, possibly, technology • Open enrolment of pupils • Records of achievement for 11–12-year-olds
September 1991	• Programmes of study, etc., for 8–9-year-olds in mathematics, English, science and, possibly, technology • First assessment of stage-1 pupils	• Programmes of study, etc., for 13–14-year-olds in mathematics and science • Programmes of study, etc., for 12–13-year-olds in English and, possibly, technology

demonstrates that headteachers, their colleagues and their school governors are already involved in managing multiple change and that this will increase in complexity and scale over the coming years.

The changes are not simply technical. They embody values that are highly controversial, professionally as well as politically, as a more analytic summary of the main features of the government's strategy indicates:

- The establishment of a framework of national objectives, standards and priorities for schools and LEAs.
- The redistribution of power by decentralizing as many decisions (e.g. on finance and the hiring and firing of staff) as possible to schools, while requiring LEAs both to support and to evaluate schools within the national framework of objectives and standards.
- The creation of a market-oriented culture for schools whereby clients (parents) are empowered (through increased powers for governors, open enrolment, access to published assessment scores and the possibility of opting out of LEA control), to choose which schools to support; and whereby schools are compelled to compete with each other for their clients and thus, in theory, to raise their standards of teaching and student learning, by using their financial, human and physical resources more cost-effectively.
- The requirement that the LEA should hold school heads and governors accountable for the planning and delivery of the national objectives and standards by evaluating and inspecting their work according to specified performance indicators.

Thus, the task of managing simultaneously multiple and complex innovations now dominates the professional lives of all those involved in the education service. Moreover, these changes have to be managed alongside the ongoing work of maintaining standards of teaching and learning as part of the normal routine of school life. Headteachers and their staff have little previous experience upon which to draw in facing a challenge of this scale and pace. It is clearly essential that effective management development and support is provided for them if these reforms are to be effectively implemented. As the leader of the government's School Management Task Force put it:

> Better schools rely ultimately on a confident and competent teaching force. Teachers have the right to expect well-managed schools which provide the conditions for good teaching and learning.
>
> Heads and senior staff have the major responsibility for creating these conditions. They too need support, especially through this period of change and reorganisation. There is an urgent need for training to prepare them to manage the many elements of reform. Beyond this, the education service needs a sound framework for systematic training and development which will support heads and senior staff throughout their careers and prepare their successors.
>
> (Styan, 1989, p. 1)

A major aim of this book is to assist LEAs to adopt a more systematic approach to school management development within a coherent framework that is based upon their strategic development plan. However, in the short term LEAs are, understandably, giving the highest priority to the task of providing heads and senior staff with the information and skills they require to manage the various parts of the reform. A recent NDC survey of LEAs in England and Wales concluded that:

- Most LEAs are concerned about the management problems faced by senior staff because of

the sheer number and speed of changes facing their schools and their inability to provide enough support to give senior staff adequate preparation for effective implementation of these changes.
- A large minority of LEAs perceive a need for training in the management of specific innovations, most notably local financial management and appraisal.

(Wallace and Hall, 1988, p. 7)

The risk is that LEAs will adopt an approach that lacks both coherence and consistency of purpose, and that the training for one part of the reform will overlap with, or even duplicate, other training. This would obviously be both expensive and inefficient. One serious consequence, which is already evident, is that of INSET overload: many headteachers are now resisting the withdrawal of yet more staff to attend INSET courses because of the disruption caused to teaching and learning. A related problem is that many LEAs have been prompted by the 1986 and 1988 education legislation to reorganize and to change the responsibilities of advisers to meet the increased requirements for monitoring and inspection. It is not always clear who should be responsible for supporting school management development. Yet, notwithstanding the urgent need to provide consistent training in support of the implementation of the Education Reform Act, LEAs must also adopt a longer-term plan for integrating a coherent and systematic management development strategy into their reorganized support structure for schools. Further-education lecturers will also require management development, though their needs are not dealt with in this handbook.

The government's School Management Task Force (Styan, 1989) proposed broad principles for a national framework that generates three key questions for LEAs:

- How much management development and training might all heads and senior staff reasonably expect as an entitlement?
- How can the various partners – LEAs, schools, DES, providers and professional associations – give practical expression to their corporate responsibility for promoting good management development?
- How can individual heads and senior staff be encouraged to give practical expression to their personal commitment to self-development?

We would suggest an additional one:

- What kind of professional values should good management development embody and promote?

There can be no simple response to these questions. Each LEA will produce different answers in the light of its own context, climate and culture. We merely want to endorse these as important underlying questions and to offer a framework within which they can be considered.

Following this introductory chapter, the book falls into three main sections:

Chapters 2 and 3　Chapter 2 argues the need for coherence and consistency in school management development, and for an LEA policy. Chapter 3 suggests ways in which LEAs can check on their current position and decide on one of two strategic approaches to improvement.

Chapters 4 and 5   These chapters outline the first option – an *ad hoc* approach to the improvement of school management development. Chapter 4 concentrates on the improvement of management training, education and support, and ways of supporting school-level programmes. Chapter 5 suggests ways of broadening the range of techniques used to promote management learning. The suggestions in both chapters can be taken up by advisers, inspectors, officers and trainers meeting as individuals or in groups: they are not dependent on the existence of a broader policy framework within the LEA.

Chapters 6 to 9   These chapters outline the second option – a more systematic approach to the improvement of school management development, based on the assumption that an LEA policy decision has been taken to move in this direction and that the chief education officer (CEO) had designated a co-ordinator with LEA-wide responsibilities for school management development. Three improvement stages are proposed:

1. Initial review (Chapter 6).
2. Priority projects (Chapter 7).
3. Overview and re-start (Chapter 8).

Chapter 9 outlines case studies of these stages in action.

Chapter 10   Finally, Chapter 10 draws some broad conclusions about school management development as a major innovation in LEAs.

Practical examples and suggestions are included throughout. Some of them may seem obvious, but our experience is that what seems familiar and obvious to one person or to one LEA may be quite new to others – LEAs have different policies, problems and priorities and are at different stages with respect to school management development.

2

THE NEED FOR A COHERENT AND CONSISTENT LEA POLICY ON SCHOOL MANAGEMENT DEVELOPMENT

The main management task facing schools is the management of multiple change, as Table 1.1 (p. 4) indicates. Thus, the most urgent short-term task for LEAs is to ensure that their numerous and diverse dissemination and training activities for heads and senior staff (on such topics as the local management of schools, appraisal, the national curriculum and testing, TVEE, school development plans, etc.) have coherent and consistent aims, avoid duplication of content and are delivered as cost-effectively as possible. Yet, when faced with a large agenda for change, LEAs and schools understandably give priority to disseminating information and giving teachers training in the basic skills required to implement each particular innovation. Furthermore, innovation-related needs may become the sole priority to the exclusion of all others (e.g. improving selection procedures). This can result in a rather incoherent approach that ultimately may be unsatisfactory and rather ineffective.

The Need for Coherence and Consistency

The need to establish some overall coherence may seem obvious, but the scale of the task should not be under-estimated. Some of the practical issues involved in achieving coherence can be illustrated from the experience of representatives from several LEAs who set out to tackle them in the context of a workshop seminar. Having reached some broad agreement about what they meant by management development and training, the group then reviewed experience in each LEA. Located in outer London, LEA 1 has a population of 319,000. It has 23 secondary schools, 100 primary schools, 41,300 pupils and about 2,300 teachers. It has an advisory and support service staffed by 30 inspectors and advisers who are responsible for about 250 advisory and support teachers (an unusually high number), all working on various aspects of staff development and school improvement. In 1988–9 these staff were responsible for 16 major curriculum and related projects, with a total budget of £1.7 million derived from a range of Education Support Grant, LEA and private foundation sources, and involving most schools in the LEA. In addition, under the LEA Training Grants Scheme, £880,000 was spent on 26,000 training days. These total budget figures include the salary and other costs of support staff and central administrators. Yet management development and training was going on under several budget headings, organized by many different people, and it often resulted in duplication and overlap. The background was a strong tradition in the primary sector of one-term and 20-day training, and a series of four-day courses for heads based on an industrial management centre, followed by a series of one-day courses on aspects of management run by LEA staff and then by training for TVEI, appraisal and LMS. It was relatively unco-ordinated, but a former secondary head had been appointed as Principal Adviser for Management Development and Appraisal. Her key initial tasks were to review current approaches in the authority and to produce a coherent management development programme, possibly based upon some notion of entitlement, all within the LEA Training Grants Schemes framework.

The background in LEA 2 was that there had been a well-established training course in senior management for primary and secondary heads, which had recently been extended to secondary-school deputy heads and heads of departments and to deputy heads in primary schools. However, these courses were being discontinued because of a number of developments, including the decentralization of INSET budgets to consortia and the appointment of staff development officers in each secondary school who were given 20 days training over an 18-month period. The consortia now included primary INSET representatives. There was also an established induction course for heads and a course on managing school review for representatives from every primary school. Existing provision was relatively unco-ordinated – it lacked back-up trainers when key people left and there was a lack of in-school support. A management-training steering group had recently been established, chaired by the staff inspector for INSET. It included representatives from the LMS, appraisal and national-curriculum training teams together with college providers. Its aim was to co-ordinate provision and make best use of the money from the different budgets. A new training course would consist of a generic or core component, currently being tested with heads, covering basic skills in management together with a series of 'satellite' modules that were topic specific. Thus, the core course might include material on discussion and interview techniques, classroom observation, report-writing, monitoring and evaluation, and the 'satellite' course on appraisal would relate these directly to the appraisal process. Training-support materials were currently being produced. The approach was exciting but posed major resource and logistic problems.

In LEA 3, all schools were required to produce an institutional development plan (IDP) each September, and heads, deputies and advisers had a two-day workshop on this subject. The IDP was intended to assist schools to implement the Education Reform Act within the framework of their own aims. Staffing arrangements and job descriptions had also been reviewed. It was now proposed that everyone with a promoted post must carry a responsibility for people management. This had clear implications for line-management structures and appraisal. Job descriptions had been introduced into primary and secondary schools. There were now training programmes for heads of department and primary deputies, for aspiring heads of department and for the induction of headteachers.

In LEA 4, a great deal was also happening but co-ordination was difficult. A third-tier officer had management development as part of a very large portfolio and although the planning was generally good, delivery was patchy. Management training had had a secondary bias, possibly springing from the original focus on the one-term and 20-day courses. There was a coherent management and professional development strategy in place in the authority, which involved five phases: preparation, pre-induction, induction, in-service and retirement. However, this plan was not systematically implemented largely due to lack of resources and manpower. There were also similar plans for secondary deputies including a nine-day training course with a residential component. A course for middle management included a classroom observation element linked with appraisal and one on the team and departmental review process. All primary schools had had a day on preparing an institutional development plan and in secondary schools departments had had school-based training. All schools were to have job descriptions. Plans for senior management-team training on a six-school basis lasting for a weekend was being developed.

In LEA 5, a subgroup had been established for national priority area 1 – management training. The officers were trying to co-ordinate existing provision across administrative divisions, for example, for LMS and appraisal. The aim of the subgroup was to identify the management skills common to management tasks. However, it was proving hard to develop a coherent programme – provision consisted largely of separate courses. The training programme on institutional development plans included a day on organizational needs analysis with an input on appraisal as a management tool. Advisers had developed an induction programme for heads. The possibility of a management development sub-committee was being considered.

The LEA representatives felt that they urgently needed some overall plan or strategy for management development that would pull all the various initiatives together. Some of the advantages they saw in this were the following:

- A coherent LEA management development policy and programme gives credibility to that programme and helps schools to make the right links between courses. Within schools it also allows teachers to make links with their own school management structures.
- An integrated programme avoids overlap and repetition and ensures that limited resources are used effectively and economically.
- Training for general skills promotes coherence in what otherwise may be seen as separate aspects of management, for example, questioning and listening skills are relevant to job selection, coaching, feedback and appraisal interviews.
- An integrated programme reduces disruption in schools and classrooms by ensuring that repetitive courses are avoided.

They suggested that the approach they were seeking would have these features:

1. The LEA would have a clear overall LEA development plan analogous to the schools' institutional development plans. This LEA development plan would be based upon a consultative process involving the participation of all key interest groups in the authority. Schools and heads would then have a clear idea of the parameters of their own institutional development and of the head's targets.
2. The LEA would also have a clear management development policy and plan arising from the overall LEA development plan.
3. The LEA would have established a co-ordination team or structure (e.g. a steering group or team) to co-ordinate management development and training across the LEA. The structure would be flexible and dynamic enough to respond to changing needs in the schools and the LEA. For example, the outcomes and messages from appraisal, such as on resource allocation, priorities and communication blockages, would be synthesized and fed back to this co-ordination team so that they could take it into account. The main function of this team would be to develop and implement a management development strategy that was consistent with the LEA's overall development plan. Steps it might take include:

   - to carry out a review of current structures and provision;
   - to ensure that new appointments (e.g. for co-ordinating TVEE, LMS, governor training and appraisal) were consistent with the overall strategy; and
   - to develop a view of how each of these innovations affected the management of the teaching force, for example, by making it clear that appraisal should not be seen as a bolt-on activity but integrated into the overall development and training structure.

4. The LEA would recognize that people only come to an understanding of each innovation (e.g. appraisal or TVEE) by experiencing it. Whatever structures were set up would not inhibit the growth of co-ordination arrangements based on this developing understanding.
5. The LEA would also recognize that each management development activity (e.g. appraisal or LMS) must develop its own materials, expertise and experience and that only after a period of time will the co-ordinators and those centrally involved in these separate activities be able to forge the right links with each other within a coherent structure. It would realize that co-ordinators for each of these separate programmes will need induction training, which helps them to make the right connections with other management training and development activities in the LEA.
6. Experience indicates that heads may find single-topic training courses (e.g. on LMS) more attractive than general management courses but the LEA would try to ensure that each course trainer and leader was in a position to make connections with the wider context and the implications of their topic for other activities.
7. The LEA would support coherent management development at school level by:

   - encouraging heads to ensure that the school's institutional development plan was modified in the light of progress reports on each innovation;
   - recognizing that small schools pose different problems and by making the most of

· alternative strategies (e.g. clusters) and inherent opportunities (e.g. for collegiality); and

● ensuring that governors' training aims to give them an understanding of management training for each innovation and its links with other developments.

The Need for an LEA Policy

One way in which LEAs can start to bring some coherence to their provision of management development and training is to agree a management development policy that is consistent with their other policies and that reflects the authority's educational aims and underlying values. The policy could set out long-term goals as well as short- and medium-term targets. Such policies would properly be distinctive in that they would relate to the LEA's particular circumstances and needs, but they would also reflect views in the profession at large about the kind of management development experiences that should be made available to teachers. Once the policy parameters were clear and a broad direction had been set, it should be possible to identify some priority areas, work on them incrementally and, over a number of years, move towards the LEA's longer-term goals for management development.

Management development policies at national, LEA or institutional level should be flexible enough to be adapted to changing circumstances. Policies are shaped by the context in which they are developed and implemented, and this changes from year to year. The challenges facing LEAs and schools as a result of the Education Act 1988 are considerable, but it should be noted that the composition of the teaching force is changing as well. First, there are fewer teachers in the system. DES statistics for 1986–7 show that there were 464,000 teachers employed in public-sector primary and secondary schools, 37,000 fewer than in 1980–1. This is a direct consequence of a decline in pupil numbers. Secondary-school rolls are continuing to fall, though primary numbers have increased since 1986. Second, the number of male teachers has reduced from 40 per cent in 1980–1 to 39 per cent in 1986–7 (20 per cent in primary schools, 54 per cent in secondary schools), though these proportions are not reflected in the teachers holding senior management positions. Third, the number of teachers who have a degree has risen steadily: 47 per cent in 1986–7 compared to 37 per cent in 1980–1. These percentages may start to reduce with the introduction of licensed teachers. Finally, the new entrants to teaching are changing – in 1986–7 a substantial number were re-entrants. In summary it can be said that nationally the teaching force is highly qualified, experienced, predominantly female, but largely managed by men. All these factors have implications for management development policies. The profile of the teaching force naturally varies from LEA to LEA: while there are authorities with no vacant posts, a stable teaching force and few teachers under 30, there are others, especially in London and the South East, where it is difficult to fill jobs, there is a high turnover of staff and large numbers of young and relatively inexperienced teachers. LEA management development policies are likely to vary to take account of these differences.

A further important point to note is the effect of the changes in in-service arrangements. There are now five school-closure days available for in-service training each year and substantial funds are made available through the Training Grants Scheme. LEAs have overall responsibility for staff development but increasingly they are delegating a medium to large proportion of INSET funds to individual schools or consortia and allowing the school staff to design an INSET programme to meet their own needs. The school governing body has the power to hire and fire staff, and LEAs have less power than formerly in the selection and appointment processes. One consequence of all this is that the LEA will need to educate and exert some influence over teachers and governors to convince them of the importance of management development, since it cannot control resources and procedures as easily as it once could.

What are the Aims of Management Development?

We stated earlier that the ultimate purpose is to improve teaching and learning by maximizing the potential of the human resources in the LEA and its schools. Few would argue with this as a broad goal, but what might it mean in practice? Numerous studies by researchers and HMI have underlined the importance of the contribution made by senior staff to overall school effectiveness, and recent studies in the USA and England have shown that schools can significantly influence pupil achievement. Studies by Rutter *et al.* (1979) and Mortimore *et al.* (1988) have identified school processes that contribute to effective schools, including a positive climate, consistency among teachers, teacher involvement in decision-making, purposeful leadership and high expectations. It can be argued that one aim of a management development programme should be to encourage teachers to adopt these effective practices. For instance, if an LEA wished to promote shared responsibility and joint planning among senior management teams in secondary schools it might give some priority to training in team-building and joint problem-solving. A related aim might be to try to maximize the amount of time that headteachers and senior staff spend on key managerial tasks as opposed to the more routine administrative work. A technical solution to this would be to increase the number of clerical and administrative support staff in schools, but teachers may also need training in delegation and time management. A recent survey of secondary deputy headteachers (SHA, 1989) showed that a large proportion of them spent time on tasks that could possibly be delegated, for example, litter collection, graffiti removal, ordering and distributing stationery, as well as the strategic managerial tasks of curriculum planning, staff development, etc.

What is Meant by a Coherent School Management Development Policy?

An LEA that is adopting a coherent systematic approach to management development will need to integrate and co-ordinate action on a wide variety of fronts, for example:

- overall educational policy and goals for the LEA;
- records and data on the teaching force;
- needs-analysis arrangements;

- innovations with implications for management development, for example, appraisal, LMS, school development plans;
- management training (e.g. short courses);
- management education (e.g. secondments and long courses);
- management support (e.g. recruitment and selection procedures, retirement and re-deployment arrangements);
- school management development policies and programmes; and
- budgeting and planning of management development within the overall INSET budget.

Co-ordination is necessary to ensure that a coherent approach to management development is followed across the LEA, that training is not duplicated and that management training and education feature in the LEA's INSET provision. This cannot be done unless the senior staff in the LEA have come to some broad agreement about their overall management development policy.

The staff concerned within the LEA would obviously have to be aware of their specific management development responsibilities and appropriate arrangements would have been made to ensure that the policy was carried out. Someone (e.g. chief adviser/inspector, INSET co-ordinator) would have been given responsibility for planning, implementing and evaluating the management development policy and programme within the broader INSET framework.

The LEA management development policy would balance and meet needs arising from:

- particular individual heads and senior staff;
- schools' development plans;
- groups across an LEA (e.g. newly appointed headteachers); and
- the LEA's policy goals (e.g. equal-opportunities policy, introduction of the national curriculum) and national policy goals.

The LEA would have encouraged and helped schools to establish procedures for identifying individual management development needs (e.g. through the appraisal process) and institutional development needs (e.g. through the use of GRIDS (Guidelines for Review and Internal Development in Schools) – McMahon *et al.*, 1984 – or some other school review process). It would have procedures for identifying LEA-wide needs that might include the use of surveys, group interviews and a databank profile of the teacher force.

The LEA would have recognized that the management development needs of individuals and groups may well vary significantly according to:

- their age and previous experience;
- their gender and/or ethnic group;
- school type (i.e. primary, secondary, etc.);
- their job stage, in other words:

  the preparatory stage (when they are preparing to apply for a new job);
  the appointment stage (when they are selected or rejected);

the induction stage (e.g. first two years in post);

the in-service stage (e.g. 3–5, 6–10, or over 11 years in post);

the transitional stage (i.e. promotion, re-deployment, retirement); and

● the specific demands of their job.

One LEA set up a working party (or Priority Project Team) to produce a policy statement. What follows is the result. It is included as an illustrative example since each LEA's policy will necessarily reflect its own particular circumstances and needs. (Note that this policy was drawn up before appraisal for teachers and headteachers was introduced.)

Example 2.1   A draft LEA policy for management development

Management development is the systematic building and enhancement of management skills at all levels of the service. In this paper particular emphasis is placed upon the requirements of those with top and middle managerial responsibilities in schools.

Skilled management endeavours to:

a. train staff systematically for leadership both in their present roles and posts for which they may wish to apply in the future;

b. help a management team to achieve a singleness of purpose;

c. develop an environment where all members of staff identify with the aims of their school and institution and care about its progress and welfare through their group commitment;

d. share expertise through in-school training, shared teaching and planning experience in order to widen the skills of all members of staff;

e. continually review methods of teaching to develop and enhance teaching styles, patterns of organisation and staffing. Institutions can thus be maintained as friendly, invigorating places in which to learn and in which the needs of individual children can be met;

f. create and develop initiatives to improve and refine the curriculum;

g. use resources effectively, fairly and efficiently;

h. build up a spirit of mutual trust and interdependence between the school, the local community and supportive agencies;

i. develop systems of monitoring and evaluation of the overall work of the institution.

Aims of the Management Development Policy

a. There should be a systematic development of skills for management of staff in the Education Service through training courses, planned experiences and continuous review of existing job functions.

b. The Authority should seek to establish a system of mutually agreed regular personal reviews of all management staff, in order to motivate staff, assess training needs and improve the quality of the education service; each person's training, experience and skills should be identified and recorded.

c. Each person's skills and knowledge should be continuously developed in order to broaden the base of skills available for the conduct of the Education Service.

d. .Opportunities for training in order to meet the identified needs of the education staff should be provided.

e. Opportunities should be sought to share management experiences, as appropriate, across all sectors of the education and other local authority services.

Objectives for Management Development

Objectives for the Management Development of Headteachers

a. A review of current activities of headteachers should be carried out with a view to identifying those functions which the Authority feels are appropriate to the task of school management. A detailed job description should then be drawn up for the role of the headteacher, relevant to the particular tier or school.

b. Each headteacher should undergo an annual review conducted by appropriate officers. The review should consider the extent to which the headteacher has been able to fulfil the demands of the agreed job description and identify areas for further personal development.

c. Each headteacher's skills, experiences and training should, by mutual agreement, be identified and recorded.

d. All headteachers should be able to take advantage of appropriate opportunities for staff development. The importance of the induction and retirement phases of a headteacher's career should be recognised.

Objectives for the management development of deputy headteachers and senior staff in schools

a. A detailed job description should be provided to each person occupying a senior management role in a school.

b. The management tasks of senior personnel should be reviewed to ensure close coordination of roles with the headteacher and other senior staff.

c. Each member of staff exercising a management function should undergo an annual review coordinated by the headteacher. The review should consider the extent to which the member of staff has been able to fulfil the demands of the job description and identify areas for further personal development.

d. The skills, experiences and training of each senior member of staff should, by mutual agreement, be identified and recorded.

e. All senior staff should be able to take advantage of appropriate opportunities for staff development. The importance of the induction and retirement phases of the career of a senior member of staff should be recognised.

Objectives for the management development of education officers

The prime purpose of management development of all officers in the Department of Education is to improve the quality of the educational experiences provided for pupils and students.

a. Each officer should undergo an annual personal review conducted by senior officers. The review should consider the extent to which the officer has been able to fulfil the demands of a realistic and mutually agreed job description and should identify areas of further personal development.
b. Each officer's skills, experience and training should, by mutual agreement, be identified and recorded.
c. All officers should be able to take advantage of appropriate opportunities for staff development.

Implementation

To achieve the aims and specified objectives, a number of steps need to be taken. These include:

a. the compilation and updating of records of relevant expertise, experiences, achievements and inservice training of all members of staff;
b. the establishment of regular reviews (preferably six monthly) of all members of staff with senior management responsibilities;
c. the provision of a coherent and relevant planned management development programme in each of the tiers of education;
d. the encouragement of institution-based programmes.

Some 2,000 staff (excluding headteachers) are involved in leadership and management posts. Management training is costly and time-consuming. Given the available resources, it is recommended that each senior manager is offered the equivalent of five days' training per year for specific management development. Each headteacher should be offered, in addition, a one-term secondment for each seven years of service.

Resources

Establishing records, reviews and programmes for management development will require the following resources:

a. appropriate staff cover to release teachers for internal or external courses and experiences;
b. the provision of appropriate accommodation with adequate resources and staffing to cope with training needs of this magnitude, consideration being given to the need for the nomination of a management development coordinator;
c. administrative staff to facilitate the recording of needs, programmes, training and experiences.

Modus Operandi

If the LEA intends to provide an overall policy to realise the aim and objective of this paper, a number of groups will be required to plan the means for implementation. These will include:

a. a group to consider a computerised record system;
b. a group to work out the aims and methods involved in a regular review of management development;
c. a group to consider how a management development programme could be planned;
d. a group to establish the criteria for institution-based training.

3

DECIDING ON THE STRATEGIC PLAN

A successful school management development scheme at LEA level depends in large measure upon the commitment of the LEA's senior staff. A strategic plan can have wide-ranging implications for selection and appointment procedures, in-service training, staff deployment and management, etc., and the management development programme will need resources and someone to co-ordinate it. Given that approximately one-third of the teaching staff have formal managerial responsibilities, a decision to focus on management development could generate many additional tasks. It is essential, therefore, that the senior people in the LEA are supportive and that the discussion about whether or not to move towards more systematic management development starts at a high level in the authority (e.g. between CEO, chief adviser/inspector and/or senior adviser, INSET).

Three key first steps are suggested for the CEO, senior officers and senior advisers:

1. Assess your current overall position.
2. Decide the broad aims and scope of the LEA strategy.
3. Decide how to manage and implement this strategy.

These three steps are intended to be carried out quickly. Experience indicates that they can be completed during two meetings.

Step 1: Assess the LEA's Current Overall Position on Management Development

The characteristics of four levels of work on management development are outlined in Table 3.1, and though these are broad generalizations and will not fit any LEA exactly, officers should be able to locate their own authority on the table. NDC experience indicates that the majority of LEAs are at level 2 and that few have reached level 4.

The questions in Checklist 3.1 are also intended to help you locate the LEA's

Table 3.1   LEA-wide management development: what level have you reached?

Level	Main observable features
1.	The LEA: • makes little management training provision of any kind for heads and senior staff (e.g. short courses); and • makes small use of management education secondments and long courses.
2.	The LEA: • makes considerable use of internal and external management training and education courses and secondments but on an *ad hoc* basis without any clear policy framework; and • is only becoming aware of the 'development' approach.
3.	The LEA: • has been working for several years on the evolution of a management training policy related to school improvement; • has a varied, vigorous and well-established pattern of activities that consist mainly of training and education courses; • is strengthening courses in terms of preparation and follow-up; • has sent most heads and senior staff on a course and some officers and advisers; • has established among officers and advisers and senior teachers a reasonably common understanding of the possibilities and limitations of training; and • realizes the need to adopt a development approach.
4.	The LEA: • has a coherent and well-publicized policy for management development aimed at school improvement; • ensures that it respects equal opportunities, especially in relation to gender and race; • has procedures and staff to implement the policy in the form of a regular programme; • makes use of job descriptions, appraisal interviews, questionnaire surveys and other methods of diagnosing needs at individual, school and LEA levels; • encourages a varied range of management training, education and support activities and uses off-the-job courses as only one component in the programme; • has the infrastructure and personnel capable of supporting course participants during the preparatory and follow-up stages and of relating such courses to the identified needs of the LEA and its schools; • encourages heads, senior staff, advisers and officers to engage regularly in the programme; • ensures that the programme is systematically monitored and evaluated in terms of school inprovement; and • ensures that the programme embraces the recruitment, selection and appointment procedures and that both governors and members are aware of this and of the overall policy.

position on Table 3.1, and to decide how and when to move forward on management development. For example, if you have no adviser for INSET or management development, who will initiate and co-ordinate any work in this area? Will this be an additional task for someone, or is it possible to make a new appointment or to second someone to take resonsibility for it? What kind of consultative procedures should be established and should this be a necessary first step? Consider finally how extensive the LEA staff development programme is and what proportion of the resources has been allocated to management development and training. If, in the past, very little has been done (i.e. the LEA is at level 1), you may not be ready to start preparing a systematic strategy. The most sensible first step might be to send a number of headteachers and advisers on external courses and so extend the group of people who can contribute to the discussion about management development and training with knowledge and experience. An LEA that locates itself at level 2 may decide to concentrate on strengthening its use of external courses by improving the ways in which participants receive preparation and follow-up. An LEA at level 3, on the other hand, may decide to devise an explicit strategy in order to bring coherence to its existing, possibly diverse, practice, and to relate it more directly to the authority's general education-policy goals.

Checklist 3.1   Basic questions about an LEA's current approach

1. What is the level of provision of school management development?
2. How is the management development programme currently funded (e.g. LEATGS, ESG, TVEE, other)?
3. How does the present approach contribute to the LEA's overall strategic development plan for education in the authority?
4. How are management development needs identified?

   - Individual (e.g. appraisal)?
   - School (e.g. school self-review/IDP)?
   - For groups of staff (e.g. questionnaires to heads)?
   - Arising from LEA innovations (e.g. LMS, school reorganization)?
   - In relation to equal opportunities (e.g. gender and race)?

5. How are the management development activities planned?

   - By an INSET or management development adviser?
   - By officers?
   - By the advisory team as a whole?
   - By a group (e.g. phase advisers for primary)?
   - On a divisional basis?
   - By individual advisers on an *ad hoc* basis?
   - By consortia leaders?
   - By individual schools?

6. How are relevant interest groups consulted?

   - heads and teachers;

- professional associations;
- elected members and governors;
- higher-education providers;
- non-education providers (e.g. local authority, industry and commerce); and
- HMI.

7. How are activities:

- co-ordinated or not?
- supported (e.g. preparation and follow-up arrangements)?
- monitored?
- evaluated?

8. Is the recruitment and appointment process appropriately integrated with the management development strategy?

All LEAs are doing some management development and training and, hence, all have at least an implicit policy. An NDC survey (Wallace and Hall, 1988) showed that the vast majority of LEAs now make some arrangements for the co-ordination of their management development and training activities and that a large minority either have or intend to develop a written policy. It may be that progress is varied and that, for example, while a great deal of management development has been provided for secondary headteachers, little or nothing has been done in the primary sector. Similarly in large LEAs there may be differences in provision of management development between particular areas or divisions.

The matrix shown in Figure 3.1 can be used to plot the current position, taking into account the answers to Checklist 3.1.

Level \ Sector	Primary	Middle	Secondary	Special	Area/Div. 1	Area/Div. 2	Area/Div. 3
1.							
2.							
3.							
4.							

Figure 3.1   Matrix to plot current position (Checklist 3.1)

Step 2: Decide the Broad Aims and Scope of the LEA Strategy

Having agreed what is the LEA's present position on management development, consider what level you aim to reach in the medium and long terms. The two approaches suggested in this book are both incremental ones that recognize that LEAs cannot work on all aspects of the school management development policy and programme simultaneously. We recommend that senior staff should identify longer-term goals and a strategy for achieving them in an agreed period. The ongoing programme can then be maintained while incremental improvements are made. The whole management development process and policy should be kept under review within the context of the LEA's overall INSET-planning cycle. Ultimately, both approaches are aimed at level 4 and thus to help LEAs establish a more systematic approach to management development and training. Both approaches will have certain consequences. For example, someone will have to co-ordinate the work, and more adviser and officer time will have to be allocated to the management development strategy. The questions in Checklist 3.2 should help you decide how you wish to proceed.

Checklist 3.2   How do you intend to proceed?

1. How should school management development contribute to the LEA's overall strategic development plan for education in the authority?
2. What priority will management development have in the LEA's overall staff development plan and budget? How much money and officer/adviser time will be allocated to it?
3. Do you intend to start with the whole LEA or a part of it (e.g. a division/area)?
4. Do you intend to start with all or only some phases (i.e. primary, middle, secondary, special)?
5. Do you intend to start with all or only some groups (i.e. heads, deputies, middle managers, etc.)?
6. Do you intend to start on all or some of the activities? For example:

   - improving courses by strengthening preparation and follow up?
   - strengthening the equal-opportunities aspect of the selection and appointment process?
   - promoting school-based support activities?

7. Which strategic approach is preferred and feasible given the climate and culture of the LEA?

   (a)   An '*ad hoc*' or 'organic' approach?
   (b)   A systematic approach?

The most important question in this checklist is the first one. School management development is not an end in itself: it is a means to the improvement of teaching and learning. Hence, it is crucial for the CEO and his or her senior colleagues, perhaps in consultation with elected members, to clarify the implications for management development of the LEA's overall strategic development plan. Prior decisions about the LEA's plan for the introduction of the national curriculum and assessment, LMS and appraisal, for teacher recruitment, for TVEE and for a host of other initiatives, should determine the broad aims and scope of school management development in the LEA.

The two broad strategic options posed in question 7 of Checklist 3.2 form the basis of the rest of the book. It will be apparent that the distinction is somewhat artificial. Certainly the *ad hoc* approach could lead into a more systematic approach to the improvement of school management development in an authority. Nevertheless, experience indicates that LEAs who see themselves as being at levels 1 and 2 (Table 3.1) often find it easier to adopt the *ad hoc* approach and, for example, to concentrate on improving training first. LEAs at level 3, however, may prefer to concentrate on a more systematic strategy from the outset.

Step 3: Decide how to Co-ordinate and Implement the Strategy

Whichever strategy is adopted, and certainly for the systematic improvement option, an early task is to agree how this work should be co-ordinated. Ideally, a senior person who has access to the key decision-making groups would become the co-ordinator, and one or more people could be designated as assistants. For example, the co-ordinators have included a deputy CEO, a senior adviser in-service and a chief adviser. One authority set up a management develoment unit with a seconded deputy headteacher as full-time co-ordinator. This latter approach obviously increases the amount of time the individual can spend on management development work; the risk, however, is that if he or she is not a regular member of the key decision-making groups it may be more difficult to ensure that a management development perspective informs all aspects of the LEA's work. Since the job will involve co-ordinating all the authority's management training activities (whether they are funded under LEATGS, and ESG or TVEE) into a coherent programme, the person doing it will need to have credibility, status and good interpersonal skills.

We recommend that you identify a small number of people to form a core management development team with the co-ordinator. The reason for doing this is not merely to share tasks but to widen the group of people who understand and are committed to the emerging management development policy. The composition of this group will vary from one LEA to another but it would normally involve someone from each of the main sectors – primary, secondary or special – and would include the advisers/inspectors with main responsibility for INSET, and for key innovations with implications for management development (e.g. appraisal, TVEE). If the LEA has a divisional structure, consider whether work should begin in one or more divisions and select members for the core team accordingly.

The co-ordinator and core team will need clear terms of reference. In other words, they will need to know the scope of the task, what outcomes are expected and how much time is available. It is crucial that co-ordinators know to whom reports have to be made, who should be consulted and informed and how much authority and freedom to operate they have. It is a very useful exercise to draw up an outline timetable and set some clear deadlines. For example, if the task is to produce an LEA policy document on management development for heads and senior staff across the authority, it may be advisable to set the deadline to coincide with the major committees who will need to approve it. If the policy has resource implications (as it undoubtedly will) it needs to be available for discussion before the INSET submissions for the following year are prepared. Consider whom else should be consulted and informed (e.g. providers, professional association representatives, elected members) and agree how to do this. You may wish to begin relatively informally and establish a formal management development advisory group later.

Five of the LEAs who worked with NDC on management development established some form of management development advisory or steering group (see Example 3.1). The characteristic feature of these groups was that they all involved some practising headteachers. In some cases the group included representatives from industry. For example, one set up an advisory committee 'composed of both experts in the field of management development and representatives of schools who could benefit from this expertise'. The major purpose of the committee was 'to provide a policy statement for the county setting out clear priorities in the area of management development. It would also assist in the identification of expertise outside the education field which could usefully be drawn upon'. A second LEA set up two management development advisory groups, one primary, one secondary. They would join to discuss broad policy issues but then break down to discuss the specific management development needs of heads and senior staff in the different sectors.

Example 3.1   Brief for an advisory management development steering committee

---

(Membership: headteachers, LEA advisers, representatives from local providing agencies and teachers panel.)
   The tasks before the panel are:

a. to consider present practice in management development and training;
b. to assess the effectiveness of present policy and practice and to identify major gaps;
c. to identify those existing elements which should be maintained;
d. to make policy recommendations to the authority for management development.

A further preliminary task is to provide the necessary support mechanisms for co-ordinators – at minimum a desk, access to a telephone and secretarial support. If they are to convene meetings they will almost certainly need a small budget. When the co-ordinator is an adviser already in post, this may not be perceived as a problem, but if a new appointment is made it is essential that these support mechanisms are available. Location is important: for example, a co-ordinator who is a seconded teacher based in a teachers' centre will almost certainly find it harder to contact advisers and officers than one with an office in the education department.

An important underlying dilemma is that although we have argued that senior officers in the authority must be committed to the strategy, this commitment requires a corresponding allocation of time and resources. Experience has shown that a CEO cannot realistically set aside time to co-ordinate management development on a day-to-day basis; it may also be problematic even for a deputy CEO to do this. Senior officers and advisers need to make a realistic assessment about the extent of their own participation and make arrangements to keep themselves informed if they cannot be involved in the core management development team.

4

AN *AD HOC* STRATEGY I:
TRAINING, EDUCATION AND SUPPORT

Improving Management Training

In the short term, LEAs will undoubtedly want to concentrate on providing management training to support the implementation of the Education Reform Act. Within this short-term framework, the following possibilities should be considered:

- For many of the reforms, heavy use will probably be made of the so-called 'cascade' method. In essence, this involves a national project or agency promoting awareness-raising through national conferences and a range of resource materials aimed at key LEA staff, who in turn make analogous arrangements for key school staff, who then run some school-based events. Although this approach was much criticized in relation to GCSE, it is one of the best available methods of large-scale dissemination. It is particularly good for raising awareness about new developments and for briefing key people with basic information. Hence it is a key component during the early initiation phase of an innovation but it is a weak method for training people in new skills.
- During the implementation stage it is vital that effective training in new skills is provided. Many LEAs have tackled this successfully by establishing in-house training teams. Once trained themselves – an essential first step – these teams are in a good position to provide support through a variety of training methods that are aimed at improving skilful performance, and that take place as close to the job as possible (include on-the-job 'coaching') and that are reinforced with follow-up support and 'top-up' training. (These techniques are described in Chapter 5.)
- Distance learning and open-learning materials (e.g. videos, tape-slides and handbooks) are valuable supplements to both the cascade and in-house training-team approaches. In particular, they considerably improve the consistency with which information about the innovation is communicated and understood.

- Another successful mechanism for support during the implementation stage is for LEAs to create networks and consortia for information exchange, collaboration and mutual support using action-learning sets and peer-coaching. Sometimes a network can be relatively formal, as in a consortium, but they can be more loose and informal. However, they are much more likely to be successful if they are given LEA support in the form, for example, of formal recognition, some secretarial help and facilities to enable members to meet. Headteachers, deputy heads and middle managers invariably express appreciation of such networks.
- Some training should focus on mixed groups of heads, governors, officers, advisers and members. New roles, relationships and forms of partnership will have to be forged and mixed-group training will assist these changes, as well as promoting consistency of purpose.
- Consistency of purpose is more likely to be achieved, school managers are more likely to be supported and the cost-effectiveness of the training is likely to be improved if the training focuses explicitly on both generic and specific management knowledge and skills. Wherever possible the knowledge and skills common to several or all management tasks (e.g. communication, interpersonal and team-building skills) should be presented so as to emphasize their general applicability and should be offered to a wide range of middle and senior managers. On the other hand, those that are more task specific (e.g. 'accountancy' skills in LMS) should be tackled differently and offered primarily to those who need them. In order to do this, each of the main managerial roles for implementation of, for example, the national curriculum and testing, appraisal, GCSE, TVEE and LMS, should be analysed in terms of their key tasks and the skills needed to carry them out. Common and distinctive aspects of the tasks can then be distinguished and so too can the general and specific skills needed. In this way the implications for specific and general management training should be clarified.
- The distinctive challenge of the Education Reform Act for headteachers and their senior management teams is the management of multiple change. This involves:

  - managing the introduction of each innovation;
  - managing the innovation during implementation; and
  - managing all innovations and all ongoing work at the same time.

The tasks involved should be clarified and the techniques and skills needed to carry them out should be the focus of training.

One priority must be to make better use of our present knowledge in order to provide effective management training and education courses. The suggestions here focus mainly upon external short courses because they are the most frequently used and often the most expensive type of management training. If they are to be cost-effective (i.e. in improving performance, rather than in simply providing a satisfying professional experience) they have to be planned carefully by all concerned. Ideally they should be planned by the LEA and the provider (who could, of course, be an LEA adviser as well as an external trainer). The experience of the one-term and 20-day school management courses was illuminating in this context. Although many of the participants' early criticisms were directed at the courses themselves, these diminished significantly as the 'teething troubles' were sorted out by course organizers and tutors. However, criticisms directed at LEA sponsors have continued to the present. They may be summarized as:

- a lack of rigour in the process of selection and preparatory briefing, linked to the absence of a clear LEA training policy. Too many participants still say, 'I only found out I was coming on this course two days ago' and, 'I don't know why I'm here. I was just told by the LEA adviser on the phone that I should turn up';
- an overuse of awareness-raising lectures, located in the training institution;
- a lack of training in specific skills directed at performance improvement;
- an insufficient attention to solving participants' work-related problems in school;
- a lack of 'on-the-job' follow-up support, particularly by LEAs; and
- superficial internal course evaluations that do not attempt to measure the impact of training on managerial performance in school.

Rooting Courses in the LEA's Management Development Philosophy

The relationship of courses to the LEAs' policy on management development should also be considered. If external courses, and indeed the whole professional development process, are to be effective, then certain basic requirements are essential. Each school should have a policy and programme that balances:

- the development needs of individual heads and teachers (as identified, for example, in an appraisal process) with
- the development needs of the school or college as identified in an institutional development plan (for example, as a result of using GRIDS or some other school review process).

Similarly, each LEA should have a policy and programme that balances the needs arising from:

- particular heads and teachers;
- groups with similar needs across the LEA (e.g. women returners);
- schools' development plans; and
- LEA policy goals (e.g. profiling and school amalgamations) and national policy goals.

Following the identification of needs in these or other ways, decisions can be made about whether or not external courses are appropriate.

Consultations with Higher-Education Providers

LEAs have always negotiated with external providers when they wanted to influence the shape and content of management training courses delivered by them. Given that the LEAs are now the paymasters, external providers are even more keen to consult with them. Where this is the case one might reasonably expect:

- discussion/consultation between representatives of the LEA and providing institution about the LEA's identified management training needs and ways in which these could be met;
- opportunities for ongoing negotiation about the programme (e.g. through LEA representation on a course steering committee); and
- suggestions/practical help from the provider with selection and preparation and follow-up for courses.

Of course, a number of LEAs have used their own in-house trainers to run courses but many of the points listed here would still apply.

An LEA checklist for improving long external courses and for use as the basis for discussion with providers is given in Checklist 4.1.

Checklist 4.1   An LEA checklist for improving long external courses (including award-bearing courses)

---

1.   Course Oversight

A course steering group should be set up to:

1.   provide an overall direction and rationale for the course;
2.   agree the general course design;
3.   monitor progress; and
4.   initiate, receive and approve the internal valuation.

This steering group should include representation from:

1.   the LEAs for whom the course is designed;
2.   practising teachers within these LEAs;
3.   the providing institution, including the course director(s); and
4.   the non-education sector.

2.   Course Direction

The providing institution should designate a named:

1.   course supervisor from the full-time staff of the providing institution; and
2.   course director(s);

and should also make available appropriate secretarial assistance, within the budgetary framework.

3.   Aims and Objectives

Each course proposal should have a clear statement of aims and objectives which are:

1.   acceptable to the steering committee; and
2.   realizable within the constraints of staffing, time and resources.

4.   Content and Methodology

The course should:

1. reflect the needs of the LEAs and the course members individually and collectively;
2. enable the course members to acquire the knowledge, skills and attitudes to manage better within their own schools/departments/groups;
3. include some consideration of management development in the non-education sector, and other sectors of education;
4. employ a methodology that is congruent with the aims, objectives and content of the course;
5. recognize the need to promote experiential learning and encourage the practical application of what has been learnt; and
6. respect equal opportunities, particularly in relation to gender and race.

5.   Structure

The course should include, wherever possible and appropriate:

1. units of sustained work in blocks of continuous time; and
2. at least one residential block of not less than two days.

6.   Staffing, and Resources and Budget

The course should include, where appropriate:

1. input from

   (a)   full-time staff of the providing institution;
   (b)   school practitioners, including course members; and
   (c)   practitioners in the non-education sector and other sectors of education;

and should be:

2. appropriately resourced and accommodated (e.g. secretarial and reprographic resources should be readily available to participants, who should not be expected to use the resources of their own schools).

7.   Selection

1. The criteria and procedure for the selection of course members should be explicit and acceptable to the regional and local steering committees.
2. The target group for the course should be clearly identified.
3. There should be a further selection procedure that involves in negotiation the provider, the LEA and the prospective course members as a result of which some form of negotiated contract should be agreed.
4. The selection procedure should respect equal opportunities, particularly in relation to gender and race.

8.   Preparation and Follow-Up

There should be both preparatory and post-course support including:

1.   pre-course discussion between participant and adviser;
2.   pre-course discussion between participant and course director;
3.   a post-course unit/day organized by the provider;
4.   a post-course de-briefing between participant and adviser;
5.   LEA-supported local action-learning groups where appropriate; and
6.   opportunities for on-the-job coaching and assistance.

9. Evaluation

There should be a clear and explicit evaluation procedure with the following features:

1.   The steering group should initiate the evaluation, well in advance of the start of the course, appoint the evaluator and agree the terms of reference.
2.   A proportion of the course budget should be set aside for evaluation.
3.   The course should be evaluated against its aims and objectives, immediate and long term.
4.   The draft evaluation report should be presented to and considered by the steering group.

Selection for Courses

Selection procedures would be improved if:

- needs had been clearly identified;
- LEA advisers (or whoever is selecting participants) clarified exactly who should be the target audience for the activity and agreed some criteria for selection;
- the course literature made the selection criteria explicit;
- it was made clear when the LEA intended that every teacher in a particular category should have an opportunity to participate in a particular activity (e.g. every second-ary headteacher should attend a 20-day management course);
- records were kept so that it was possible to check which teachers have or have not participated in a particular activity or programme;
- selection interviews were conducted when appropriate;
- selection procedures were standardized and co-ordinated across the LEA; and
- the process was monitored to ensure that it respected equal opportunities.

Pre-Course Preparation

In themselves, courses, no matter how well conducted, are a weak mechanism for bringing about change. Without careful preparation and follow-up, the likelihood that they will have some lasting impact is even further reduced. When the course is 20 days or longer this must be a matter for serious consideration. All too frequently teachers attending management courses complain that they are not sure why they have been selected by their LEA and that they have not been given a clear brief about what the course will involve. Effective pre-course preparation can include:

- the LEA and provider clarifying the purpose and target audience for the course;
- careful selection of participants well in advance of the start date;
- negotiation with colleagues/head;
- opportunities for participants to do preliminary work/preparatory reading that will be discussed on the course;
- the LEA making clear its expectations for the participant and the follow-up that will be provided;
- a joint pre-course meeting between LEA adviser, course director and participants from that LEA; and
- the course director visiting participants in their schools before the course starts.

Effective Training and Coaching

In outline, emerging theory argues that individual learning and organizational change requires a range of development, training and learning approaches; that the traditional external course, while reasonably effective as a briefing device for promoting awareness, is poor at promoting behavioural and organizational change; that these are more likely to be achieved through techniques that are specifically aimed at particular learning targets, which should themselves be rooted in the individual's practical tasks and experience; and that development and training should take place as close to the work situation as possible. Fundamental to this emerging theory is the belief that, although professionals should be supported to acquire a repertoire of techniques and skills, in the final analysis they are frequently required to exercise them in complex, dynamic and unpredictable situations for which specific training cannot be provided. Thus, the concept of reflective practice is a useful one in understanding these dilemmas and in helping the trainers and practitioners to resolve them.

In a seminal paper, which is nevertheless still insufficiently known and used in the UK, Joyce and Showers (1980) outlined a theory of skill training based upon a review of US teacher-education research. They distinguish between two aims for skills training – the 'fine-tuning' of existing skills and the learning of new ones – arguing that the former is easier to achieve. They go on to distinguish between four potential levels of impact that, adapted to school management, are as follows:

1. General awareness of the new skills.
2. Organized knowledge of the concepts and theory underlying the skills.
3. Learning of principles and skills ready for action.
4. Transfer and application of the new skills to the school and integration into the management repertoire.

Not unreasonably, they argue that only when level 4 (point 4 above) has been reached should any impact on the school be looked for or expected.

They also distinguish between five principal training methods or components:

1. Presentation/description (e.g. via lecture/discussion) of new skills and underlying theory.
2. Modelling the new skills (e.g. via live demonstration or video).
3. Practising the new skills in simulated and controlled conditions (e.g. with peers or with small groups of staff).
4. Feedback on performance of new skills (e.g. using a structured system/instrument or unstructured discussion) in simulated and/or real settings.
5. Coaching for application, transfer and integration via in-school assistance from peers and from trainers.

The essentials of their theory, illustrated in Table 4.1, are embodied in the paper's concluding paragraph (p. 384–5):

> if any of these components are left out, the impact of training will be weakened in the sense that fewer numbers of people will progress to the transfer level (which is the only level that has significant meaning for school improvement). The most effective training activities, then, will be those that combine theory, modeling, practice, feedback and coaching to application. The knowledge base seems firm enough that we can predict that if those components are in fact combined in inservice programs, we can expect the outcomes to be considerable at all levels.

Table 4.1 Learning new teaching skills

Training method/ component	Level of impact			
	A. General awareness of new skills	B. Organized knowledge of underlying concepts and theory	C. Learning of new skills	D. Application on-the-job
1. Presentation/ description (e.g. lecture) of new skills	✓	✓	✓	✓
2. Modelling the new skills (e.g. live or video demonstrations)		✓	✓	✓
3. Practice in simulated settings			✓	✓
4. Feedback on performance in simulated or real settings			✓	✓
5. Coaching/ assistance, on the job				✓

In subsequent work (e.g. Joyce and Showers, 1988), these ideas have been tested and evaluated and they have concluded that the use of coaching can significantly improve transfer of learning and that teams of peer 'coaches' should be trained.

Post-Course Follow-Up Support

A major purpose of follow-up support is to ensure that expertise acquired on a course can actually be used to benefit the school or LEA. That this does not always happen is evidenced by the following example. The One-Term Training Opportunities (OTTO) programmes were originally intended to include a 'training the trainers' component – it was envisaged that this would enable the participant heads to 'train' other headteachers and senior staff. Yet several headteachers who attended these courses subsequently found that the LEA expressed no interest in the skills they had acquired and understandably this was a source of considerable frustration.

The following methods have been used by LEAs to provide follow-up support:

- An opportunity for a participant to have a debriefing session about the course (e.g. with LEA adviser/officer).
- On-going support in implementing strategies/techniques learned on the course.
- The LEA indicating how it plans to use individual expertise gained on the course.
- Use of 'critical-friend' technique back on the job (see Chapter 5).
- Visit from adviser/advisory teacher.
- Follow-up meeting of participants to review action plans.
- Network of supportive colleagues.
- Evaluation meetings to discuss impact on practice.
- Action plans for group of schools.
- Combined in-service/curriculum development meetings.

Using 'Trained' Teachers as Trainers

LEA advisers have increasingly become managers rather than deliverers of in-service training. Schools need help in identifying and meeting management development needs, and participants for in-service courses and activities require preparation and follow-up. Some ongoing consultation with providers will probably be necessary and working on these tasks is likely to be a more effective use of an LEA adviser's time than running an in-service course. Since it is likely that there will be a shortage of management development trainers, LEAs need to explore ways of using the expertise of its headteachers and senior staff (see Example 4.1).

Experience suggests that:

- teachers should not be expected to become trainers without receiving some appropriate training themselves and ongoing support (e.g. regular discussion and problem-solving related to their work as trainers);
- if individuals are being used as trainers on a withdrawal basis (e.g. coming out of school one or two days a week) the demands made on them should not be such that their school suffers;

- supply cover should be made available when required (e.g. when the head is acting as an LEA trainer); and
- the LEA should monitor and evaluate the work of its trainers.

Example 4.1   *Using experienced heads as trainers*

Four LEAs collaborated to plan and support a 20-day management training programme based at the local university school of education. A member of the university staff acted as supervisor of the programme. However, it was directed and run on a day-to-day basis by two headteachers seconded from each of the four LEAs in turn. These two headteacher trainers were selected from the participants in the one-term management training programme run in the previous year. The 20-day course had a steering committee and an evaluator.

Improving Management Education

Experience in both education and industry indicates that management education is essential to the development of effective management capacity. Management education includes secondments, attachments and fellowships, lasting from one term to one year and full- or part-time courses leading to an advanced diploma or a masters degree in a university or polytechnic.

Many in-service advanced diploma and M Ed courses include a specialism on educational management and administration. Most courses, whether full- or part-time, include a project that may relate to each student's job, and study for a degree by research may be based on an investigation into some aspect of school management practice. The skills developed for study of this kind relate to some of the skills required by managers: for example, the ability to analyse, create new ideas, manage time effectively and write a precise, logically argued report. Study of the theoretical bases of management practice raises awareness of the complexity and dilemmas of school management, giving students the conceptual tools to analyse their practice. There is a long history of award-bearing courses as a basis for personal development. Chances of promotion are seen by students to be favoured by attaining such awards. But the award generally refers to a high standard of reflection, investigation and writing about practice, not to actual performance of management tasks in school. As a management development activity, the award-bearing course should meet an identified need that will result in some impact upon performance, however indirect.

A fellowship or attachment is an opportunity for individual study, normally lasting one term or more, based with an institution providing in-service training. In addition to expert supervision given by a tutor, fellows have access to resources such as a library, and contact with others with similar interests. As a management development activity, a fellowship should combine personal development with an aim – however indirectly – to improve management in the fellow's school or across the LEA. The topic for investigation is negotiated between the individual and the LEA responsible for the fellow's secondment, in consultation with the providing institution, which has expertise in areas such as methods of investigation and knowledge of relevant literature. A fellowship may be conducted by a single individual identifying, for example, management development needs amongst a section of the LEA's teaching force, such as heads of small primary schools, secondary-school deputies or heads of departments. Several fellowships may be set up in the same LEA, following each other or at the same time, so that fellows may support each other and make a particular contribution towards a different part of the LEA's policy. Fellows might, say, identify management development needs among different sectors of the teaching force or examine management development needs arising from innovations initiated by the LEA. Individuals from neighbouring LEAs may collaborate through a networking arrangement, possibly co-ordinated by a local providing institution (see Wallace and Butterworth, 1987). The criteria used to select teachers for fellowships should be related to the task, so, for example, if the LEA wants the outcome to be a written report it is often sensible to select someone who has recent successful experience of writing (e.g. a dissertation for B Ed or M Ed).

Since the introduction of the LEA Training Grants Scheme in 1987, there has been a substantial drop in the take-up of both full-time secondments and longer, award-bearing courses. This is understandable given the pressures on LEA and school INSET budgets but it is, none the less, to be regretted. LEAs and professional associations should clearly and unambiguously acknowledge that secondments and award-bearing courses are essential to the effective management of schools and the health of the education profession.

There are three main reasons for this view. First, a range of education and training options should be available if LEAs and schools are to make meaningful choices. Second, and more importantly, short courses do not provide sufficient opportunities for sustained, in-depth work on the complex tasks of school management. Third, and most importantly, it is in the longer-term interests of children and society to have heads and senior staff who, whilst always working within the law, are capable of making independent, critical and informed professional judgements, and not simply to have functionaries who carry out the policies of a particular employer or government unquestioningly. Advanced, professional, management education is one of the best ways of ensuring that this happens.

Of course, the practical difficulties must also be faced up to. First and foremost, secondments and long courses are expensive: a full-time, one-year M Ed can cost £2,000, which is a substantial sum for an LEA and which would consume the whole annual INSET budget for some schools. Second, athough advanced courses are widely acknowledged to be intellectually challenging and to enhance career prospects, they are often seen as too theoretical and as not matching up to the criterion of immediate practical relevance. For instance, many LEA officers do not think that long award-bearing courses are an effective way of improving performance.

Most LEAs are committed to support some secondments and long courses but the rationale for this is usually implicit and vague. A first step, therefore, is to develop a clear policy on management education. Checklist 4.2 may help LEAs to do this.

Checklist 4.2   Developing a policy on management education

1. What percentage of the LEA's INSET budget is spent on secondments and long, award-bearing courses related to school management? How does this compare with similar LEAs? Should it be modified?

2. How are staff selected for such secondments and long courses? What are the criteria, procedures, policy framework and priorities? How do these compare with similar LEAs? Should the approach be modified?

3. How are the outcomes and benefits of secondments and award-bearing courses evaluated? What are the benefits? Should the evaluation procedures be strengthened?

4. How extensive is the range of providers used by the LEA – local, regional, national? Are the programmes offered on a 'take-it-or-leave-it' basis, or are they jointly negotiated? How does this LEA's approach compare with others? Should it be modified?

5. Is the LEA taking steps to negotiate with universities, polytechnics and colleges of higher education to ensure that their advanced diploma and M Ed courses are modified along lines such as the following:

    (a) Much greater emphasis on general and specific knowledge and skills (e.g. local financial management, appraisal, staff development, the management of change).

    (b) Greater emphasis on reflective practice (e.g. via action learning, action research, case studies, project-based assignments).

    (c) More frequent use of distance-learning materials and of collaboration with the Open University and the Open College.

    (d) The adoption of modular structures and of credit accumulation and transfer using the UCET and CNAA schemes.

    (e) More systematic evaluation of individual courses and overall specialist management programmes.

    (f) The introduction of skills-based and performance-based qualifications involving assessments that focus less on written work and more on the work-based performance of skills taught on the course. These could be assessed by, for example, colleagues and advisers who had been trained for the job, on the analogy in initial practice of the joint assessment of teaching practice by school staff and college tutors.

6. Is the LEA making the best use of secondments and fellowships, for example, by using some type of formal agreement or contract between the LEA, the provider and the seconded fellow? (A possible format is set out in Example 4.2)

Example 4.2   Pro-forma for an agreement on seconded fellowships

The written agreement will be based upon the following information:

- Fellow's name
- Position
- Home address and telephone number
- Work address and telephone number
- Period of Fellowship
- Name of LEA sponsoring Fellowship
- HE Institution Supervisor   Telephone Number
- LEA Contact Person for Fellow   Telephone Number
- Fee
- Fellow undertakes to: (major tasks, detailed outcomes and target dates)
- HE Institution undertakes to: (standard/extra facilities)
- The LEA undertakes to: (tasks connected with Fellow's work)
- Other notes

An extract from a completed pro-forma reads as follows (a primary head was given a one-term secondment to produce some management-training materials for use with other primary heads meeting in cluster groups):

Fellow undertakes to:

Tasks • develop and trial management training materials on one topic for use in clusters
- devise a suitable process for the development, trial and dissemination of materials by others
- report to the LEA on that process
- produce one set of materials for dissemination

Outcomes and Target dates

1. Proposal for draft materials – 12th September
2. 1st draft of materials for trial – 15th October
3. Redraft and trial with one cluster group – 24th October
4. Proposal for amendment of materials – 3rd November
5. Amendment of materials and dissemination to all clusters – 24th November
6. First draft of report on process (to include the set of materials as appendix) – 1st December
7. Final draft presented for typing – 15th December
8. Up to 30 copies of report produced by the HE institution and delivered to LEA – 1st February.

The HE institution undertakes to:

- provide supervision – up to $10 \times \frac{1}{2}$ days
- provide a room, desk and telephone

- provide secretarial support for supervised work
- provide access to its resource bank
- provide access to its contact network
- produce up to 30 copies of report

The LEA undertakes to:

- set up and service cluster groups among primary schools throughout the LEA for the management development activities
- facilitate the development of materials to be used by cluster groups for management development, without external support
- provide an LEA contact person for the Fellow
- set up a steering group to include LEA and HE institution representatives to review progress made by Fellow
- arrange up to three meetings of the steering group during the period of the Fellow's secondment.

Improving Management Support

By management support is meant those job-embedded activities that are an integral part of the manager's job. Many of these ideas and techniques have emerged from industry and commerce and hence they should be adapted to education with care.

Management Recruitment, Selection and Promotion

Large firms regard the selection of managers and planned succession as being fundamental to an effective management development policy. In its pure form, this approach is not possible in education because school governors are now responsible for the appointment and dismissal of staff, including the head and senior staff, whereas the LEA is responsible for the development and training of staff. Planned management succession is ruled out when these two functions are separated. The difficulties are further compounded because most of the governors are non-professional lay-people whereas the responsible LEA officers are all professional educationists. In practice, therefore, LEAs should aim to create a 'pool' of developed and trained personnel from whom school governors can select their managers when posts become vacant. There now exists a substantial body of practical and research-based knowledge about the selection of headteachers and deputies (see Morgan, Hall and Mackay, 1983). The implications for the training of governors are also considerable.

Job Descriptions

The process of drawing up, negotiating and implementing job descriptions is both a way of clarifying the work of each member of a school staff and an opportunity for practice in communication, consultation and decision-making that is directly relevant to people's jobs. Job descriptions may take various forms, commonly consisting of a brief statement of the job-holder's role or title – curriculum adviser for art and craft or deputy headteacher (curriculum development), for example – followed by a more detailed list of tasks for which the person is responsible. For managers, this should concentrate on people-management tasks. Where job descriptions do not already exist, the first step is often to analyse what each staff member actually does, followed by discussion of what each person should be doing and the boundary of their responsibility. In a primary school, for instance, the curriculum specialist for art and craft may be expected to order and stock the materials that colleagues use. A boundary of the curriculum specialist's responsibility may be that he or she is not expected to cut up materials ready for colleagues' lessons. Once agreed, written job descriptions can form a basis for the appraisal process, in the light of which, individuals' development needs may be identified, jobs and their boundaries may be renegotiated, and individuals may try out different responsibilities (see Boydell, 1973; Ungerson, 1983).

Appraisal

In industry, performance appraisal is the systematic evaluation of individuals' performance in their present job and their potential for development. Generally, each person in a management hierarchy is interviewed periodically by a senior manager to whom he or she reports. The interviewer and the subordinate together review the goals that the latter has been trying to achieve, analyse critical incidents that have happened since the previous appraisal interview and set new goals for the subordinate. Judgements are based upon explicit performance standards. Many schemes have three elements: the reward review, which relates to salary, influence and status in the organization and job satisfaction of the person being appraised; the potential review, which predicts the kind of work the person will be capable of doing in the future, how long he or she will take to achieve this and what preparation may be required; and the performance review itself, which addresses the need to improve performance of the present job and highlights needs for training. In order to ground the interview in subordinates' self-appraisal, interviewers must be able to perform various skills of interviewing including active listening and counselling.

Following the nationally funded pilot schemes in six LEAs, a national framework for the appraisal of all teachers, including headteachers and senior staff, was drawn up. This has many features distinctive to education but, crucially, appraisal is seen both as a key management tool and as integral to management development (see DES, 1989).

Job Enrichment

A job may be replanned in order to make the tasks involved more challenging for the person involved. Job enrichment may be employed as a way of encouraging staff development in general, and development of staff in their management responsibility in particular. The first steps are to identify what the present job actually entails and what the person doing the job needs to learn in order to develop. Job enrichment may consist of a greater number of tasks to be performed at the present level of responsibility. For example, a primary-school curriculum adviser for science may also take on additional responsibility for environmental studies. New tasks may be undertaken at a different level of responsibility: a secondary-school teacher may take over the requisitioning of stock from the head of department. Often job enrichment includes a combination of tasks at the same and different levels of responsibility.

Job Rotation

A planned programme of job rotation consists of two or more people spending a period in each other's jobs. Often the group involved in a rotation scheme undertakes a number of jobs at the same level of responsibility as a way of broadening experience. Rotation may be part of the process by which individuals may develop themselves in preparation for possible promotion to a post with greater management responsibility. In planning a job rotation exercise, it is important to identify the nature of each job and the development needs of the people involved. For instance, the deputy headteachers in a large secondary school may exchange specialist responsibilities, or a school deputy may become acting head while the headteacher is on secondment, a head of department may act as deputy, and so on. The opportunity to try out in practice, however temporarily, a post carrying a higher level of management responsibility, is a powerful way of learning to perform new tasks in preparation for possible promotion.

Support for School Management Development

A great deal of management development must of necessity take place on the job in school. Our definition distinguishes between management training, education and support and while training and education might be provided by the LEA, many support activities can only take place in school. Schools will need to develop management development policies and programmes that are congruent with the LEA policy. In the main, this is a task for the head in consultation with staff and governors; nevertheless, the majority of schools would benefit from external help and advice at various stages. This can most readily be provided by the LEA, though occasionally it might be supplied by an external consultant or trainer. Some strategies for supporting school management development are listed below. (The two companion books in this series offer more detailed ideas for schools themselves.)

Disseminate Information about Management Development

Many teachers will be unfamiliar with the concept of management development; some will dislike thinking of themselves as managers. Anything that the LEA can do to promote discussion about what a management development programme might involve will be valuable. Possibilities for doing this include discussion at headteacher meetings; sending draft policy statements to schools for discussion; identifying people who can speak about management development to staff in schools; and making training materials available to schools for use on training days.

Provide a 'Vision' for School Management

The LEA can make a valuable contribution by initiating and contributing to a debate about how schools might or should be managed. School management development programmes are intended to make individuals and groups of teachers better managers but frequently the philosophies and values that underpin such programmes are left implicit. A head may not share them with staff in the school, let alone with staff in other schools across the LEA. So, for instance, if the LEA advisers and officers feel that the head and deputy headteacher should operate as a close team, that decisions should be taken in as open a manner as possible, that all teachers should have an opportunity to express their views on major items of school policy, that as many decisions as possible should be devolved to middle managers (e.g. responsibility post-holders), then these are issues that they can put forward for discussion and debate.

All have profound implications for the way teachers fulfil their managerial role and so for the management development programme. The process of producing the school's development plan offers an ideal opportunity for such a discussion.

Allocate Resources to Management Development

A very tangible form of support the LEA can provide is to allocate LEATGS and other resources for management development. This would require them to earmark a proportion of the in-service budget for management development and training and ensure that, whether the money was held centrally or was given to consortium or to individual schools, it was spent on management training and support activities as intended.

Support for School Management Development Co-ordinators

In the early stages when schools are drawing up management development policies and extending their programme of activities, the LEA can provide several kinds of very practical help for school management development co-ordinators. To begin with an LEA adviser can recommend to the head that he or she acts as co-ordinator or designates another teacher to do the job. Once a co-ordinator is in place, an adviser can provide individual advice and suggestions for action during visits to the school and he or she can also organize occasional meetings for all the co-ordinators in a particular group of schools or across the LEA. Such meetings can provide an invaluable opportunity for exchanging information and ideas. The LEA might even arrange some specific training for co-ordinators if this seemed necessary.

Provide Access to Materials

The LEA might establish a central information resource bank of management training materials that individual schools could use. Examples of such materials would include commercially produced videos, examples of management self-development activities, key reference books, exemplar questionnaires that might be used for needs identification, evaluation, etc.

Provide Advice and Facilitate Networking between Schools

As well as building a resource bank of materials, the LEA (or more specifically the person acting as LEA management development co-ordinator) could usefully build up a databank of information about management trainers, consultants, local-authority personnel, industrialists, etc., who could usefully support management development in school. This would mean, for example, that a school that wanted someone to run a session on team-building or that wanted some information about how selection and appointment procedures were handled in other schools, could fairly quickly be given the name of someone they might turn to for advice.

5

AN *AD HOC* STRATEGY II:
BROADENING THE RANGE OF MANAGEMENT
LEARNING ACTIVITIES*

Management development is more than courses: we have suggested in previous chapters that it encompasses a wide range of on-, off- and close-to-the-job activities, and outlined some of the more widely used techniques. In this chapter a number of additional activities LEAs and management trainers might want to employ are described. Those responsible for organizing and delivering management training, education and support may find it useful to reflect upon and extend their repertoire of methods and techniques. They might, for example, ask themselves, how wide a range of methods and techniques do I employ? How flexible am I in my approach? When did I last try out a different technique (e.g. for organizing group discussion)? Would I benefit from a 'training-the-trainers' programme? If I feel that I would benefit from some further training, how can I acquire this?

This chapter provides details about some less familiar activities and is arranged alphabetically. Since most activities may be used in various situations by people with different background experience and expertise, no attempt is made to indicate levels of difficulty. Some activities are likely to be straightforward, others may be sensitive and therefore require preparatory work to foster the conditions necessary for successful implementation. Selection should be made with care. The activities are defined so as to encourage clarity, and specialized terms have been kept to a minimum. The activities and methods are all intended to support learning and they may be interpreted, combined and modified through use; in some cases, there is a degree of overlap between them. The directory could never be complete as new methods and ideas are being devised and tried out all the time. The activities presented here may well stimulate the development of new ways of supporting management development in schools. A

* This chapter is based upon extracts from Wallace, 1986.

comprehensive source of activities and associated reading is Huczynski, A. (1983) *An Encyclopedia of Management Development Methods*, Gower, Aldershot.

Action-Centred Leadership

This term refers to a view of leadership developed by John Adair. Where a task must be achieved by a group, leadership should be adaptable to match the constantly changing situation. For a team to be successful three types of need must be met. Task needs cover the necessity of achieving the tasks; group needs refer to the degree of co-operation between team members that is required; and individual needs are those personal needs that each individual seeks to fulfil (such as the need for self-esteem). Leaders must see that all three types of need are being met.

The approach is learned through action-centred leadership courses. A set of group tasks is given and feedback is provided on members' performance in relation to meeting the needs, issues of communication and the problem-solving approaches used by the group. Courses are normally centred away from participants' jobs. Action-centred leadership courses for heads of school are offered by the Industrial Society (see Adair, 1979 and 1984).

Action Learning

This is an approach developed by Reg Revans on the assumption that managers learn to perform most effectively by tackling and solving real work-related problems. Groups of managers from the same or different organizations, who are facing broadly similar problems, come together periodically to work on their problems in a learning 'set'. Each set includes a 'set adviser' who acts as a facilitator and resource person, aiming to develop the set so that the practitioners learn from each other. Between meetings of the set, individuals work on their own 'project', attempting to solve a management problem they have identified.

In the set, mutual support is given for each person to analyse his or her problem by asking searching questions. Strategies are developed to solve the problem, including analysis of the resources that would have to be procured. Resources are assembled and the solution is implemented by each person back in the job in the form of some kind of managerial action. Finally, the effectiveness of the action implemented is evaluated in the set according to the questions originally raised in defining the problem. This review may lead to the raising of new questions, so beginning another action-learning cycle. A number of variations of this model have been developed outside and within education.

Action learning has been adapted for use in external school management training courses. Participants, usually from different schools, help each other to plan an intervention in each person's school. By the end of the course, participants will have made action plans they intend to implement afterwards on their return to school.

Where the course consists of several blocks of days spent in the set interspersed with periods in school, it is possible for participants to implement their action plans in school and to review them in the set during a subseqent block of the course. Action-learning sets could be organized for, say, heads of department in a large secondary school or among heads of neighbouring primary schools (see Revans, 1972 and 1984; Pedlar, 1983; Wallace, 1988).

Action Research

Action research means a careful and thorough enquiring into a problem that includes taking action to resolve it. A report is made so that others may learn from the experience. In school management, one or more individuals may take such a rigorous approach towards their performance of management tasks. The aim is to improve their performance by raising awareness of a management issue or problem in the school, then planning and taking managerial action.

The process consists of a cycle. First comes planning. In the light of a general idea about an issue (such as communication problems between staff), fact-finding provides a deeper understanding and informs discussion and formulation of an action plan to improve the situation. Second, the plan is implemented, involving an assessment of the effects of the action. Third, the action is evaluated through a review that leads to a new understanding of the situation and the beginning of a second cycle. Other practitioners in management positions may find it useful to learn about the process, and a report, often rendered anonymously, is also a way of making sure that the action research is carried out rigorously.

This approach towards the improvement of one's own practice has been most fully developed in schools in relation to work with pupils, but it is being applied to work with adults. A head may, for example, conduct action research into his or her role in facilitating communication between staff (see Elliott, 1978; Day *et al.*, 1985; Hopkins, 1985; Wallace, 1987; McNiff, 1988).

Assertiveness Training

Assertiveness means being open and flexible, genuinely concerned with the rights of others, yet at the same time able to establish one's own rights firmly. The basic goal of assertiveness is to stand up for one's basic human rights without violating those of others, and the aims of assertiveness training are to enable people to learn the skills needed to interact effectively with others without being aggressive or being dominated by others, to be self-confident and to be an effective member of a work team. Verbal skills include the ability to repeat one's wishes calmly to others and non-verbal skills include the establishment of eye contact.

Training programmes may help participants to assess their own behaviour and to practise the skills of assertiveness through role-play exercises. Such activities might, for example, be undertaken by teachers with management responsibility as part of an external training programme (see Langrish, 1981).

Brainstorming

This is a simple way of ensuring that, within a group, each person is able to contribute ideas about the topic under discussion and, as a problem-solving technique, it enables the group to consider the fullest range of solutions. A procedure may be used to group ideas together and to select or reject ideas, according to the task in hand.

The process is based on all participants following certain ground rules. First, everyone in the group is invited to contribute as many ideas on the topic or problem under consideration as they can think of, however far-fetched they may appear to be. All ideas are recorded so that the group may see them on, say, a flip-chart. Individuals are not allowed to evaluate other people's ideas at this stage; they may only ask questions of clarification. Often, when all ideas are exhausted, the participants who offered certain ideas agree to group them together. Subsequent discussion may be structured so as to arrive at certain priorities, and to select or reject particular ideas.

Brainstorming may be particularly useful in situations in school such as a staff meeting to decide upon priorities for management development, or a senior management team discussion of a management problem. It is a technique those who have to organize discussions as part of their management responsibility may find useful to learn.

Case Studies

A case study is an account of a particular situation. One type of case study is commonly used as a component of training programmes to illustrate certain learning points. The account may be of a real or fictitious situation, and the information given is selected according to the learning focus – perhaps emphasizing school management structures or particular interactions. The case study often forms the basis of a simulation exercise. Learners' awareness of certain management issues is raised and it is often assumed that they can relate to their own context an understanding derived from another situation.

In a second form, people study an aspect of their situation in order to deepen their understanding of management in their school. The approach may be used to generate issues or problems of which the student was previously unaware, or may have an initially identified focus. Methods are various, including interviewing, observation and studying documents, and students must learn how to apply them rigorously and sensitively. Case studies of participants' own situations may form part of an external training programme as a way of broadening the evidence on which a management decision related to the school is based. The materials for the Open University course, EP 851, *Applied Studies in Educational Management*, give a comprehensive account of this approach (see Goulding *et al.*, 1984; Paisey, 1984; Lyons, Stenning and McQueeney, 1986).

Coaching/Counselling

Coaching and counselling are closely related; they refer to the process by which a person with management responsibility helps a colleague, through discussion, to learn to perform a management task or solve a management problem. The support given varies from a strongly directive form of coaching to a non-judgemental 'sounding-board' type of counselling. In the latter case, the individuals being counselled are helped to reflect upon their performance or problem, to make their own judgements, to think of ways forward and to decide upon action. Those who take on the counselling role must learn certain skills, including the ability to listen actively and to frame appropriate questions. One variant is co-counselling in which two colleagues in the same organization act as counsellor for each other.

There are many opportunities in schools for coaching/counselling activities. A head may counsel junior colleagues, or heads of department or curriculum advisers may co-counsel each other, for example (see Megginson and Boydell,1979; Reddy, 1985; Showers, 1985; Joyce and Showers, 1988).

Consultancy

A consultant is a person who offers knowledge, or expertise as a facilitator, to people in other organizations. Schools may benefit from a consultancy supporting various parts of the management development process: identifying needs and selecting, implementing and evaluating activities. An effective consultant must have learned to be skilful in collaborating with people from other organizations in situations that may be sensitive or potentially threatening, in addition to developing expert knowledge of, say, training techniques.

There are many opportunities for consultancy in the area of school management development. A school may, for example, engage the services of an adviser, a member of staff from another school or a tutor from an institution providing training. There is a wealth of expertise amongst tutors – if they are to act as consultants, schools must expect to pay for their services, possibly through an arrangement negotiated with the LEA. Within a school, members of staff with expertise may act as consultants to their colleagues. Consultants may contribute to the various kinds of external training programmes that are available to heads and senior staff (see Kubr, 1976; Beck and Kelly, 1989).

Critical Friendship

Two or more colleagues agree to give mutual support for their on-the-job learning by giving sympathetic comment to each other's managerial performance. Necessary skills include the ability to observe carefully and to ask appropriate questions and listen actively when giving feedback. Informal arrangements are made for mutual observation during, say, a staff meeting, and for giving and receiving confidential feedback afterwards. Curriculum advisers in primary schools and secondary-school heads of department may agree to comment upon each other's actions in support of their colleagues (see Mackay, 1980 and 1984).

Critical-Incident Analysis

A 'critical incident' may be defined as an event involving people in an organization, which has given rise to problems with the achievement of management tasks. In school a crisis may, for example, have developed over the allocation of the capitation allowance, or the use of the hall by different classes, or between colleagues concerned with a part of the curriculum.

Individual awareness of such incidents may be raised by keeping a 'critical-incident diary', as part of a self-development exercise. Analysis may be a group activity, conducted in school by, say, the management team or a department as part of a training programme, or an action-learning group. First, each member recalls from personal experience a critical incident connected with his or her management tasks at school. Group members give an account of this incident to each other. There may be further exploration of the incident through a role-play exercise.

A problem-solving process may be used in order to help each person develop an action plan to resolve the issues arising from the incident. Typically, each incident is addressed in turn. First, symptoms are distinguished from possible causes (conflict between staff may be a symptom whose causes may lie in the way decisions were made about distribution of the capitation allowance). Second, the group brainstorms all possible causes. Third, likely, relevant causes are selected and discussed. Fourth, as many alternative solutions as possible are brainstormed, without evaluation. Fifth, the group evaluates solutions and, sixth, the individual or group decides upon an action plan (see Lacey and Licht, 1980).

Development Training

Development training refers to small groups each of which works as a team to achieve various tasks, often based out of doors and frequently involving strenuous physical activity. The tasks are a vehicle for encouraging members to reflect upon and develop their individual and collective performance as leaders and followers. The experience may take the form of an intensive residential programme situated at a centre isolated from the outside world. Assumptions generally include, first, that individuals may develop their personal confidence, self-knowledge and leadership skills through team-work involving tasks whose relation to the normal job is that of a simulation exercise. Second, trainers are expected to transfer subsequently what they have learned to the performance of management tasks at work, often with colleagues who have not had the training experience.

Development training is widely used outside education. A few heads and senior staff are able to take part in such programmes, often forming a component of an external training programme under the special regulations. Development training using the outdoors is being incorporated in several training programmes specifically for heads and senior staff in schools (see Beeby and Rathborn, 1983; Bank, 1985).

Distance Learning

This term is used for approaches where the learner does most of the work involved in the activity away from the teaching organization. In the UK, the Open University in particular has developed correspondence courses in which students work through materials and exercises. A locally based tutor assesses and gives feedback on written assignments. Most courses may contribute towards an award. Various organizations, such as the Joint Examinations Board, offer award-bearing correspondence courses relating to school management.

Open learning is a variant where students may use packages of material flexibly, selecting topics and the pace of learning.

In the field of educational management, the Open University offers a number of courses relating to the management of schools that may contribute towards a first-degree programme or a diploma in educational management. One course (EP 851) is specifically designed for students to examine their own management practice, and the course, E 325, is on managing schools. Open University materials are available for purchase whether or not they are used as part of a course. Further details of Open University courses may be obtained from the LEA INSET adviser or from the Open University. Other correspondence courses are advertised in *The Times Educational Supplement*.

Group Memory

It is easy to lose sight of what has been said during the course of a discussion. In some group activities it may be worth while to record the point made by each participant so that the issues raised and points made may be resurrected by group members and may be retained for later analysis.

One simple method of recording is to use a flip-chart. Either one person records for the group or each participant writes up their own point. Usually a short phrase containing the key words is enough to trigger memories afterwards. At the end of the session, the completed flip-charts are available for future reference.

A 'group memory' may be valuable for most meetings in school where opinions are sought or decisions must be made. It is a useful technique those staff members who have to manage meetings as part of their management responsibility may learn.

Intervisitation

Two or more people whose workplaces are reasonably close take it in turns to visit each other at work and may give feedback on what is observed. It is also possible for a single visit to be made by one person to another workplace. Intervisitation programmes are usually structured so that the visit has a clear focus. A headteacher might visit a neighbouring head in school to observe a staff meeting and give feedback on the head's performance. Feedback may also be given to colleagues in the visitor's school. The other head may then visit to observe a staff meeting, and so on. As another example, a head observes how the distribution of the capitation allowance is negotiated in a neighbouring school and reports back to his or her staff. The other headteacher visits the school to see how the new capitation arrangement is being negotiated and is available to offer further advice.

In education, intervisitation has been developed as part of external school management training programmes, enabling senior staff to visit some of each other's schools; and it may form part of a school-focused staff-development programme. As part of liaison between primary and secondary schools in the same catchment area, senior staff may visit each other's school to ensure, amongst other things, that the management of the curriculum within the pyramid of schools is consistent for the pupils.

Planning for intervisitation must take into account the likely effect of a visitor or observer at a meeting or other event in school, and all concerned should be clear about the management development needs that will be met through the process of intervisitation (see Miles, 1959).

Job Swop

Two people, usually from different workplaces, swop jobs temporarily in order to carry out specific tasks. It is intended that the individuals will benefit from working in a new environment, and that the organizations concerned will gain from the perspective brought in by a new person.

On setting up a swop, the development needs of the participants are identified, and during their exchange, they concentrate on their development through carrying out tasks in the new situation. Someone in each organization takes responsibility for giving support and feedback to the person who has swopped job. Therefore, the job-swop arrangement must be carefully planned and managed by the organizations involved.

Exchanges of this kind may take place between staff with a degree of management responsibility in neighbouring schools. It may be easiest to arrange for this kind of exchange between individuals at the 'middle-management' level – heads of department and heads of year in secondary schools, curriculum advisers and year-group leaders in primary schools (see Mumford, 1980; Phipson and Smith, 1982).

Learning Contract

A learning contract is a statement drawn up by and agreed between a learner and the person acting as a trainer. It records what the learner will attempt to learn, how and when it will be done, how it will be evaluated and whether opportunities will be available to renegotiate the contract. In self-development approaches, people may make a contract with themselves to ensure their own commitment. Within a training group, each person may negotiate an individual learning contract. Contracts imply rights and responsibilities – a learner is responsible for carrying out the learning activities but has the right to support from the trainer. The trainer can expect the learner to try to learn, but is responsible for helping the learner to do so.

A learning contract is a way of ensuring clarity about the aims of a management development activity, and of gaining commitment to the enterprise from both learners and trainers. In education, external training courses for groups of people may meet identified individual management development needs through programmes that are based on each individual's negotiated learning contract. Individual projects or fellowships may similarly be based on a learning contract. In school, individual activities may be negotiated and clarified through a learning contract, possibly as one outcome of an appraisal interview (see Stuart, 1978).

Learning-Styles Analysis

Analysis of individuals' habitual or preferred learning styles may form part of the process for deciding upon particular management development activities, having first identified the learning needs of each person. It is assumed that different people tend to be comfortable when learning in particular ways, some being keen to jump straight into action, others preferring to be able to read, stand back and reflect.

According to Kolb (1976), learning by experience consists of a cycle. Immediate concrete experience is the basis for observation and reflection. These observations are assimilated into generalizations, perhaps using theoretical notions, from which suggestions for further action may be derived. Putting these ideas into action brings about new concrete experience, so beginning a new learning cycle. People tend to prefer to learn through one or two parts of the cycle, say, by experiment and direct action rather than reflection and analysis.

Kolb emphasizes that for effecive learning to improve performance in complex situations, individuals should go through all parts of the cycle. Therefore, it must be decided whether the subsequent management development activity will enable individuals to continue to use the learning style with which they are comfortable. Alternatively, the activity may be designed to help individuals to develop a more effective general approach to learning – learning how to learn – by supplementing their preferred style with the other parts of the learning cycle.

Two well-known methods for identifying learning styles are Kolb's 'Learning Styles Inventory' and Honey and Mumford's 'Learning Styles Questionnaire' (See Kolb and Fry, 1975; Kolb, 1976; Honey and Mumford, 1982; Smith, 1983).

Networking

A network is a way of providing informal opportunities for communication and support between individuals with similar interests, and between people with a problem and those who may be able to help solve it. A number of contacts are made, and a means is set up for others to join the network and for informing people about others' interests, experience or expertise. Then it is up to individuals whether or not to take advantage of the network. Networking is a potent way in which those concerned with educational management may give or receive support with each other's job-related problems.

Networks often include a central file of contacts and other resources: some have a telephone 'hotline' through which individuals can be put in touch with each other by a central person, perhaps located in a teachers' centre. In the USA, one principals' (headteachers') network has produced *Yellow Pages* directories of principals who are willing to offer advice from their own experience concerning particular management problems.

A network is sometimes set up as an outcome of a management training programme involving participants from different schools within a region. Heads and senior staff, LEA advisers and tutors providing training may all participate. Some networks are facilitated and supported by LEA representatives and tutors, others originate as a self-help activity amongst a group of heads and senior staff. Virtually any group of people may set up a network. For example, headteachers or deputies in the same area may help each other to solve management problems, perhaps visiting schools or holding meetings at a local teachers' centre (see Barnett *et al.*, 1984a and 1984b).

Organization Development

Organization development (OD) describes a variety of approaches, usually involving an outside consultant, which focus on changing a group or organization as a whole. Activities often include support for those with management responsibility, but the emphasis is upon improving the way in which all the people in a group or organization work together. So a team-building exercise, for instance, may be extended to all the adults working in a school. Activities may take place in the workplace or elsewhere. OD has been adapted for use in schools, and may include training activities which enhance colleagues' sensitivity towards each other.

The entire staff in a primary school, or a working group such as the senior management team in a secondary school, may be supported by a consultant in developing their interpersonal relationships. Some sessions may take place in school, others at a residential training centre (see Woodcock and Francis, 1981; Gray, 1982; Schmuck and Runkel, 1985).

Peer-Assisted Leadership

This is a structured form of critical friendship developed in the USA. Pairs of principals agree to give mutual support in each other's schools and are trained in the skills of shadowing, analysing observations and reflective interviewing. The pairs observe each other in school and give mutual feedback by conducting reflective, non-judgemental interviews about their leadership behaviour.

Pairs refine their skill in carrying out the learning cycle by repeating the observing and interviewing cycle, and attending several more training meetings spread through a year (see Barnett, 1985).

Private Study

As the terms suggests, individuals conduct a study on their own, usually away from the workplace. They may choose the topic and the pace of learning, or may engage in private study whose outcome is assessed as part of a training programme. There is a great deal of printed and audio-visual material on educational management that may stimulate individuals' reflection on their managerial work in school. As a management development activity, the focus of study arises from identification of individual needs and a major aim is to inform present or future performance of management tasks.

Quality Circles

The quality-circles approach has been pioneered in Japan where employees, usually operatives, become more involved in their work by solving their own job-related problems in an organized way. A quality circle typically consists of between four and ten volunteers from the same working group or department (not necessarily representing the whole group or department) and their supervisor or manager. The latter acts as facilitator for the quality circle, which meets for an hour each week, in paid time. Problems are identified by the individuals rather than by senior management, and are connected with their own work, not that of other groups in the organization.

Identified problems and solutions are presented to management for decisions about implementation. All members of a quality circle are given initial training in the skills of systematic problem-solving and working together in a group. The approach is adaptable to the education context. For example, quality circles may be set up within departments in a secondary school, with heads of department as facilitators (see Robson, 1984).

Self-Development

Self-development is broad concept with two main dimensions: development by the self as a process; and development of the self as a goal. Management self-development activities are usually based on a combination of both dimensions – the individual managers voluntarily engage in and control the learning process, and focus upon the goal of developing their own skills in, say, interpersonal relationships. Self-development activities tend to assume that people have a positive attitude towards learning and know how to direct their own development. A number of self-development resource packs for managers have been produced outside education. They consist typically of a means (such as a questionnaire) of identifying personal development needs or blocks to effective performance and a series of activities that can be completed alone or with a colleague or group. Exercises might include practical ways of finding out how a person spends time at work, which leads to strategies for improving the effectiveness of the use of time. Self-development materials for middle managers in secondary schools have been produced by Hall and Oldroyd (1989).

Self-development activities may be tackled by a collaborative group within the same school and have been introduced as part of an external training programme for heads and senior staff. An appraisal or counselling procedure for staff development within a school may be used to identify development needs (see Boydell and Pedlar, 1978; Woodcock and Francis, 1979; Francis and Woodcock, 1982; Local Government Training Board, 1984; MSC, 1984).

Shadowing

One person arranges to follow and observe another for a period of time while he or she goes about his or her normal job. Shadowing may be one way, for example, as a means of preparation or induction for, say, prospective or new deputy headteachers. Alternatively, two or more colleagues from the same school or neighbouring schools may arrange to shadow each other and give feedback on their observations.

The method of shadowing an experienced manager assumes that skilful performance of management tasks can be learned by observing a model manager in action. Because it may be difficult for the person shadowing to judge the relative importance of what he or she witnesses, the approach often includes systematic guidance about what to observe (see Taylor, 1977).

Simulation

Some aspect of the real world is reproduced in a simplified and controlled fashion. Participants are guided through an experience designed to highlight some of the problems of the real situation. They may have to make managerial decisions on the basis of information supplied, or engage in role play and so be protected from exposing their normal reactions.

Simulations were among the first participative methods to be employed in training programmes for educational administration and school management. They vary from 'in-tray exercises', where the trainee is presented with, say, a series of letters and memos that have arrived on a headteachers' desk, to complex management games involving, for instance, a large secondary school in which decisions made at one point lead to various consequences at the next stage. In the latter case, events and decisions that in reality take place over several years may be presented in a matter of hours. Because, by definition, the simulation experience is a simplification of what might happen in the real job, simulations may be limited in helping people to improve their own managerial performance in school; their value may lie in raising awareness and giving practice in, say, decision-making techniques (see Taylor, 1973; Taylor and Walford, 1978).

Skills Training

Skills training refers to practice (usually in a setting away from the job itself) of a particular area of behaviour, with feedback on performance. In management development, skills that individuals need to develop further are first identified then practised in a 'safe' setting, where mistakes may be made and feedback accepted without embarrassment. While it is often assumed that once practised, these skills may be directly applied to the job, further coaching may be given by observing and giving feedback on an individual's subsequent job performance.

There is a wide range of skills for which practice may be needed, depending on the management tasks that people perform. In schools, many skills are related to working with other adults, including listening, collaborative decision-making, appraising and being assertive. They may refer to general areas such as problem-solving or specific tasks such as planning, timetabling or report-writing, and may include a sequence of particular procedures or strategies.

A workshop may be set up in a school on, say, listening skills needed for conducting an appraisal interview. The group concerned may divide into pairs and each person acts in turn the roles of speaker and listener. An interview is conducted, and the listener then reports back to the speaker what has been said. The pair may subsequently agree to give critical feedback to each other while performing their job in school (see Cooper, 1981).

Stress Management

Stress arises from a combination of pressures related to the achievement of management and other tasks in the job, individual physical and mental reactions to pressure, and the coping strategies that people use to reduce or control stress. Stress may be roughly defined as reactions to job pressures that are greater than individuals' coping resources, resulting in poor job performance.

The first step in stress management is for individuals to identify and accept that they are showing symptoms of stress. The second step is to select strategies that may focus upon one or more factors, reducing pressures relating to job tasks (e.g. by delegating more to colleagues), and improving coping strategies (e.g. by developing a regular relaxation routine). The intended outcome is to change individual physical and mental reactions and so to improve job performance.

Activities for identifying stress, reducing pressures and improving coping strategies may be carried out by one person or may involve others. Individuals may undertake job-related self-development activities such as analysing how they spend their time in school or less specifically job-related activities like relaxation training, meditation or developing a hobby. Activities involving colleagues include examining job descriptions in order to achieve a better pattern of delegation, developing a critical friendship between, say, a headteacher and a deputy for mutual observation and feedback, or counselling – the head may have a wide-ranging, confidential discussion with a colleague who is showing signs of stress (see Dunham, 1984).

Structured Group Discussion

There are many ways of organizing a group discussion. As a way of identifying management development needs in a school it is important that all staff members' views are represented and that particular individuals do not dominate the proceedings. The group may operate without a formal leader.

The first task is to gain agreement on the ground rules for the process of discussion in the light of its particular purposes. It may be that a decision must be reached about priorities within the range of views expressed. If so, the process for arriving at a decision must be agreed.

In order that all views are expressed, each person may state or write down what he or she wishes to put forward. Others may not evaluate views at this stage: only questions of clarification may be asked. Each view is recorded in a group list. If individuals agree, two or more views may be grouped together. Discussion may then take place. One strategy is for each participant in turn to be given the opportunity to restate his or her case.

The final stage is to establish priorities and arrive at a decision. Each participant may rank the ideas put forward. All rankings are then listed and compared. A decision may be made according to which idea was ranked highest by most people. Alternatively, each person may vote for one or more ideas, the votes are counted and the most popular idea accepted.

Team-Building

In most organizations, including schools, the management function involves collaboration between several people. The aim of team-building activities is to develop a group of managers, each of whose work is affected by the others, into an effective team. It is assumed that a group of managers working collaboratively as a team is more effective than individuals working on their own (for some routine tasks, teamwork may not be particularly necessary). The process of building teams takes considerable time and may be approached in various ways. Examples include activities located away from the workplace, such as games designed to reveal the need for mutual trust, and structured reviews of a staff meeting at work that involves team members. Teams are seen to develop through several stages, and individuals may perform various roles within a team. There are several ways of diagnosing individual or group development needs, leading to activities to meet them and so to improve the team's effectiveness.

Many team development activities may be adapted for school-based use among those with management responsibility – the senior management team of a secondary school or the head, deputy and curriculum advisers in primary schools, for example. Working groups that include colleagues without major management responsibility, such as secondary-school departments or complete primary-school staffs, may also undertake team-building activities. Participants in external school management programmes have engaged in team-building as a means of developing mutual trust and openness at the beginning of the programme (see Woodcock, 1979; Belbin, 1981).

6

A SYSTEMATIC STRATEGY I:
THE INITIAL REVIEW

The next chapters (6 to 9) deal with the second strategic option and therefore offer certain practical suggestions for the systematic improvement of an LEA's school management development scheme. It is assumed that the CEO and his or her senior

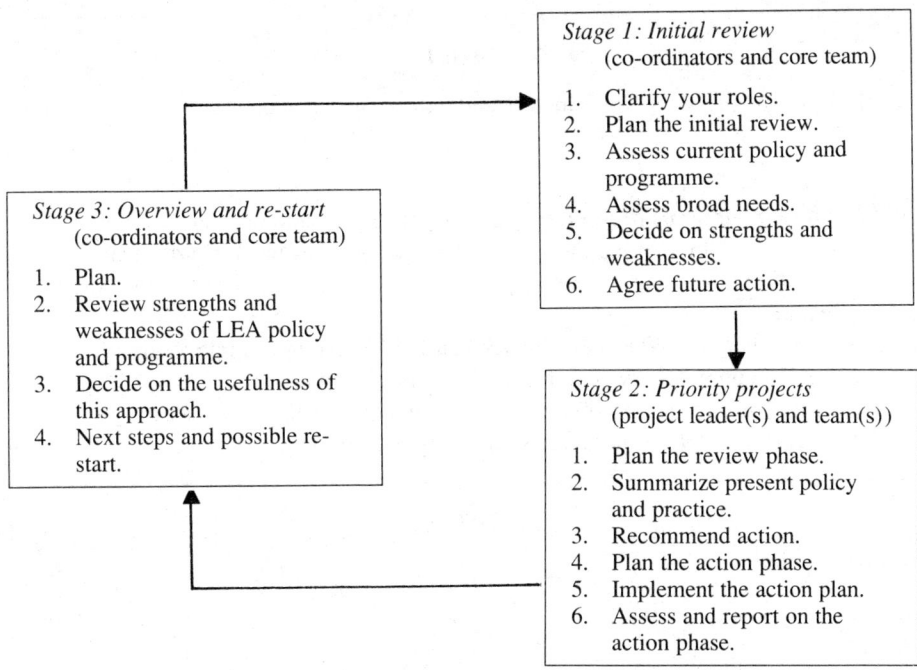

Figure 6.1   A systematic strategy for improving school management development

officers have decided to adopt this approach and that someone has been designated as
LEA co-ordinator. Three broad stages are proposed, as indicated in Figure 6.1. Each of
these stages begins with a summary of the suggested procedure, which is then followed
by explanatory comment and illustrative examples.

The suggestions in this chapter are primarily directed at the LEA management
development co-ordinator and the members of the core team (see Chapter 3). They are
intended to help you to review existing practice and to decide upon an appropriate
incremental strategy for moving forward. We recognize, first, that the LEA's ongoing
programme of management development activities will have to be maintained while
this is happening and, second, that the information you would like to draw upon may
not be easily available. The main message is to carry out the initial review as thoroughly and systematically as possible, but to use what information is readily available
rather than spend several months collecting detailed data. The initial review is intended
to help you reach speedy decisions about priorities before moving into an active
developmental phase. It should not be so lengthy and exhausting that it results in
paralysis.

The key tasks that need to be considered at the initial review stage are discussed in
Checklist 6.1. The co-ordinator will have to undertake some preliminary work but once
this is complete the main decisions can probably be taken in one or two meetings.

*Checklist 6.1   Stage 1: the initial review (key steps for co-ordinator(s)
and core team)*

Step 1

Clarify your role(s) as co-ordinators and core-team members.

Tasks

1. Check your terms of reference, the extent of your authority and on the
    procedures for keeping the CEO and senior officers/advisers informed.
2. Clarify the working relationship between the co-ordinator(s) and the core
    team.
3. Check that you have been allocated sufficient resources to do the job (e.g.
    time, accommodation, equipment, secretarial support).
4. Check with the senior officers that the support mechanisms necessary for
    successful implementation have actually been established.

Step 2

Plan the initial review.

Tasks

1. Agree a short but realistic timetable for the initial review.
2. Clarify and implement the procedures for involving/consulting others.

3. Collect the information needed for steps 3 and 4.
4. Agree on a procedure for writing a summary report on the initial review.

Step 3

Make a preliminary assessment of the nature and extent of current LEA policy and the ongoing programme.

Tasks

1. Review any relevant LEA policy statements/papers.
2. Identify the main features of the ongoing programme.
3. Summarize your conclusions.

Step 4

Make a preliminary assessment of broad needs.

Tasks

1. Identify major LEA policies and innovations and the management development needs they generate.
2. Check what major management development needs have been identified by

   (a) individuals; and
   (b) schools.

3. Check the approximate number of teachers in the management development target groups and estimate their broad needs.
4. Summarize your conclusions.

Step 5

Decide on the strengths and weaknesses.

Tasks

1. Synthesize the conclusions from steps 3 and 4.
2. Identify those features of current policy and the ongoing programme that are satisfactory and should be maintained.
3. Identify major gaps and unsatisfactory features of current policy and the ongoing programme. Distinguish between those that:

   (a) should be dealt with as specific priority projects in the short or medium term;
   (b) are better dealt with in the long term.

Step 6

Agree an incremental strategy for achieving systematic management
development.

Tasks

1. Agree the aims and scope of the strategy and a realistic timescale (e.g. one,
    three or five years) including a provisional date for the overview (stage 3).
2. Identify available resources (e.g. funding, people, agencies).
3. Identify likely barriers and ways of overcoming them.
4. Ensure that arrangements for maintaining the ongoing programme are
    satisfactory.
5. Identify the people, methods and resources required for initiating the
    priority projects.
6. Draft a summary report on the outcomes of the initial review.
7. Distribute this draft report to senior officers/advisers and others and seek
    their agreement on any recommendations for programme maintenance and
    specific priority projects.
8. Finalize the report and agree immediate next steps.

Step 1: Clarify the Role of the Co-ordinator and Core Team

The initial suggestion is that you clarify what is expected of you as co-ordinator. It may
be difficult to define the role exactly at the outset, especially if the LEA has not
previously undertaken much work on management development, but you should be
able to establish the broad parameters. The key issues are: what are you expected to
undertaken and/or produce; to whom should you report about your work; and how
should you inform other officers and advisers about what you are doing? All these
matters may well have to be negotiated with the CEO or the person to whom you have
been asked to report. A further question is the relationship between you and other
members of the core team. This is potentially tricky. For instance, if the adviser INSET
is identified as co-ordinator and the other members of the core team are the deputy
CEO and the senior advisers primary, secondary and FE, some agreement needs to be
reached about the extent of their commitment to the management development team,
their availability for meetings, whether they will be prepared to undertake information
collection or whether they see their role as being to give advice on policy, etc.

It is advisable to keep adviser and officer colleagues informed about what is happening in management development, not least because the policy that emerges may
ultimately affect their work, for example, the type of in-service courses they organize.
One suggestion is that the CEO at the outset sends a memo to inform people that the
LEA wishes to move towards a more systematic approach on management development and that a management development co-ordinator has been designated; later the

co-ordinator can report periodically to meetings of the advisory team or write an occasional newsletter.

As co-ordinator it is important to check that you have the resources to do the job and if they are not available see if they can be supplied. Where the co-ordinator is newly appointed, for example, a seconded headteacher, the case for resources like a room and telephone can probably be easily made. The difficulty arises when an officer or adviser already in post is given this job. The main problem is finding the time to do it. Busy officers and advisers cannot normally take on a co-ordinator's role unless they drop some other aspect of their work. Though some tasks can be delegated, the job of co-ordinating the management development strategy will take at least half a day a week and more realistically one day. If the co-ordinator can obtain some agreement from the outset about the time to be allocated to the job, it may be possible to block out days in the diary. Finally, it is worth checking that any necessary or agreed support mechanisms (e.g. a management development advisory group) have been established.

Step 2: Plan the Initial Review

One of our most common suggestions is that you draw up timetables and deadlines for different aspects of the work. This is a simple but effective device for clarifying how much can be tackled at any one time and for reminding everyone involved of the short- or medium-term targets. Co-ordinators should draw up a short but realistic timetable for the initial review. What is realistic will, of course, vary from one LEA to another, depending on the time available and the accessibility of the relevant information. Essentially you will need to allow time for the necessary background information to be collected and for the appropriate people to be consulted. It should be possible to complete an initial review in a term. This allows five or six weeks for information collection and leaves space for at least two policy meetings to decide on the priority areas. Finally, you need to agree how you are going to prepare a summary report on the initial review.

In what follows we have assumed for illustrative purposes that the LEA has decided to investigate management development across the authority. However, the key questions are the same if the decision has been to start with a particular phase (e.g. primary) or a division/area of the authority.

The questions we suggest you ask at the initial-review stage appear simple though they may be difficult to answer. They are as follows:

- What do we do about management development now?
- What management development needs have we identified?
- What are the strengths and weaknesses of our current programme?
- What needs are we failing to meet?
- What should be our priorities for future work, and how are we going to achieve systematic management development?

We discuss these questions in more detail below.

Step 3: What do we do about Management Development now?

This is not the time to begin a lengthy investigative study; remember the initial suggestion that you should be systematic and thorough but should use existing information. Probably the easiest way to approach the question is to ask a senior officer or adviser from each phase to record what is happening in their area. (Ideally this person will already be a member of the core management development team.) One person can look through the LEA in-service booklet and note any management development activities. It is possible that more may be happening than you think – but it will probably not be labelled management development. The list in Table 6.1 is intended to make you aware of the wide range of potential activities. Give everyone who is collecting information about present practice a copy of this list in advance. In some areas it is likely that little or no management development will have taken place; in others a great deal may be happening (see Example 6.1).

Table 6.1   Some management development activities

Off the job
- Short courses (e.g. one day)
- Long courses (e.g. 20 days)
- Award-bearing courses (e.g. M Ed)
- Modular courses
- Fellowships (e.g. one term)
- Secondments (e.g. to industry)
- Visits (e.g. to another school)
- Distance learning (e.g. Open University, Open College)
- Private study

Close to the job
- Team-building group
- School-based workshop/course
- School-based consultancy
- Selection and appointment experience
- Self-development activities
- Action-learning set

On the job
- Drawing up a job description
- Individual appraisal for development
- School self-review
- Job enhancement (e.g. acting as project co-ordinator)
- Job rotation
- Advisory visit (e.g. non-colleague or adviser)
- Pairing with peer for mutual observation and feedback
- Planned succession experiences
- Self-development activities

Example 6.1   Existing provision of management development

The picture revealed in the primary sector might be as follows:

- Five headteachers each year have attended a 20-day management course (30 now trained).
- Twelve headteachers have been on a one-term training programme.
- The two primary advisers each year run a six-day course (one afternoon a week for a term) on management in the junior school (57 headteachers and deputy headteachers have participated).
- The primary advisers as a matter of policy visit each newly appointed headteacher twice in his or her first term to provide general support.
- One head and two deputy headteachers have been seconded part time to do an M Ed course with a specialism in management.
- Six headteachers from one cluster of schools are working on management problems through an action-learning group.

Review the major initiatives that are underway. Many if not all of them will have implications for management development, but this is not always recognized because LEAs are large and complex organizations, and it is easy for activities to become compartmentalized. For example, one LEA initially made no connection between its work on management development and on appraisal. In another, a secondary head-teacher was given a year's secondment to investigate the training needs of heads but was not told that a management development group had been established in the LEA. The co-ordinator should try to note major initiatives and collect brief written accounts of what is happening in each phase so that the members of the core LEA team can be presented with the total picture when they meet.

Step 4: What Management Development Needs have been Identified?

One easy way into this task is to ask a senior person in each phase to note what they feel the management development needs are. It is useful to include people who have responsibility for particular LEA-wide programmes (e.g. LMS, TVEI), which may throw up management needs. You might suggest that each person has an informal chat with one or two practitioners (e.g. headteacher, school staff-development officer) to see if they agree with the identified management development needs (see Example 6.2).

If one person does this for each phase, then it should be possible to build up a picture of LEA-wide needs, especially those arising from individual appraisals and school development plans. However, remember the suggestion that LEA-wide needs arise from four sources:

- Individuals.
- School/college development plans.
- The profile of the teaching force.
- LEA policy and innovations.

Example 6.2   School management development needs

Continuing the primary example (Example 6.1), we could speculate that the LEA advisers identified these needs:

- Management training for all headteachers (to date only 102 of the 270 have received any form of training).
- Support and training for deputy headteachers.
- One headteacher is in difficulty and needs to be taken out of school for a time.
- The majority of primary schools need advice about how to identify INSET needs.
- The 25 small, rural primary schools have been grouped into clusters – this has thrown up management development needs for the headteachers.
- Training for curriculum co-ordinators – highlighted as a priority in several school development plans.

Before you can really consider what the priorities are you may need access to more information. One person could be delegated to identify management development needs arising from the staff profile and LEA policies. The LEA may well not have an easily accessible data-base on staff development. Nevertheless, certain information (e.g. number and types of schools) will be known to everyone. Using Table 6.2 as a guide, check the approximate number of teachers in the target groups and estimate their broad needs.

This exercise can be very revealing. In one LEA, for example, the team realized that 17 of their 35 secondary schools had appointed a new headteacher in the previous three years, yet the LEA had never instituted any form of induction programme for them. A second authority realized that two-thirds of its secondary headteachers were in their mid-to-late fifties, that they might soon apply for early retirement and that the LEA could find itself with a large turnover of staff. Almost invariably an exercise of this type reveals that women are under-represented in management positions given their proportion in the total teaching force. Similarly, where the authority has a number of black teachers, it may emerge that they are under-represented in managerial posts and are marginalized into the multi-cultural support team. In addition to the ethical questions about equal opportunities, these issues also raise two quite different questions: is the LEA meeting its legal obligations, and is it maximizing its use of human professional resources to the benefit of its students?

The final source of needs is LEA policy and innovations. Again one person could be delegated to do some work on this. The list of innovations in Checklist 6.2 is a useful starting point. Ask someone in each phase to identify the innovations that are ongoing – typically there will be about 17 in the secondary sector and 9 or 10 in the primary. Consider what management development needs these highlight. Reflect also on LEA policy. For example, is it anticipated that some secondary schools will have to close? What is the LEA timetable for phasing in particular innovations? Does the LEA plan to

Table 6.2 Estimate the number of teachers in the target groups

| | Primary | | | | | | Secondary | | | | | | Special | | | | | | Other | | | |
| | Heads | | Deputy heads | | Responsibility post-holders | | Heads | | Deputy heads and senior staff | | Middle managers | | Heads | | Deputy heads | | Middle managers | | Advisory teachers | | Consortia or project convenor | |
	M	F	M	F	M	F	M	F	M	F	M	F	M	F	M	F	M	F	M	F	M	F
Appointment																						
Induction																						
In-service																						
Transitional																						

increase the proportion of INSET funds devolved to schools? What management development needs might arise from these policies? The co-ordinator could collect brief statements from the various people involved about what they consider the needs to be. Remind yourselves of the LEA's legal obligations, especially under the terms of the Sex Discrimination Act and the Race Relations Act. These have direct implications for selection procedures, for example.

Checklist 6.2   Current innovations, policy initiatives and developments with implications for LEAs, schools and providers

Local management of schools (LMS).
National curriculum and assessment.
Staff appraisal.
Institutional development plans.
LEA and school curriculum development plans.
Curriculum-related staffing.
DES subject statements.
LEA subject guidelines.
Micro-electronics education programme/information technology.
Low-attaining pupils programme.
School–industry links.
TVEI(E).
Pastoral curriculum.
Active tutorial work/developmental group work.
Personal, social and health education.
Ethnic-minorities policy (Swann).
Travellers' children.
Equal-opportunities policy (gender).
Section 11 money (advisory teachers).
Special educational needs policy.
Gifted children.
Homework policies.
School management development policies.
CPVE (and training).
GCSE (and training).
A- and S-levels.
Records of achievement/profiles.
Transition from primary to secondary.
Outreach – home visiting.
Community education.
Education support grant projects (e.g. small primary schools) and advisory
    staff.
Governing bodies – impact of recent legislation.
Falling rolls:

closures;
amalgamations;
re-deployment;
early retirement.

Industrial action.
New salary and career structure.
CATE – teacher fellows, lecturers as teachers.
Licensed teachers.
INSET:

school-based;
post-1987 arrangements;
courses (e.g. school management).

Specialist post-holders in primary schools.
School evaluation:

HMI published reports;
LEA inspections;
School self-evaluation (e.g. GRIDS).

Specific LEA initiatives/projects (e.g. economic literacy, study skills, school libraries, timetabling).

Step 5: What are the Strengths and Weaknesses of our Current Programme? What Needs are we Failing to Meet?

This task of deciding upon the strengths and weaknesses of the current programme is probably best undertaken by the management development co-ordinator and core team in a formal meeting. There are three questions to answer:

- What aspects of the current policy and programme are satisfactory and should be maintained?
- What are the gaps and unsatisfactory features of the current policy and programme?
- Which of these features should be tackled (a) in the short or medium term; (b) in the long term?

A synthesis of the information collected about the LEA's present practice in management development should enable the group to answer the first question, as Example 6.3 indicates. This is an impressive and extensive list of activities. Questions that LEA personnel might ask when assessing this programme are as follows:

- Is there a balance between management training, education and support activities?
- Are these courses mounted on an *ad hoc* basis or do they relate to a clear policy framework?
- Are heads of department and middle managers given appropriate support?

- Have most heads and senior staff been on some form of management training course?
- Is there enough quantified information to answer these questions?
- Is there preparation and follow-up for courses?
- Do officers, advisers and senior staff in schools have a reasonably common understanding of what is meant by management development?
- How were particular activities and courses rated? What information can be gathered from the evaluation reports?

Example 6.3

One LEA identified these key features of its current programme (they are presented here in summary form – school-based activities are not included):

Secondary

Heads

1. Induction programme for new heads.
2. Annual residential senior management conference (all secondary headteachers, plus a few representative deputy heads – approximately three days).
3. Opportunities for headteachers to apply for a secondment for a one-term fellowship or award-bearing course.

Deputy heads

1. A committee of deputy headteachers that organizes an INSET programme and an annual residential conference.
2. Organized in-service for professional tutors.

Middle management

Opportunities to participate in:

1. a one-year part-time course (30 sessions) on middle management in the secondary school; and
2. a variety of other 'management' activities in the central INSET programme.

Primary

Heads

1. Induction course for new heads (usually residential).
2. Opportunity to take part in a number of residential conferences for senior management.

Heads and other staff

Opportunities to take part in:

1. teachers' centre INSET programmes; and
2. any school-based INSET programmes.

Opportunities to apply for secondment to attend:

1. management course (e.g. 20 days);
2. award-bearing course; and
3. teacher fellowship.

Special

Heads and deputies

1. Induction course for new heads and deputies.
2. Opportunities to:

    (a) attend seminars;
    (b) attend annual residential course;
    (c) join in LEA general INSET programme (i.e. for secondary or primary); and
    (d) apply for award-bearing course.

The second task is to identify the gaps and unsatisfactory features of the present programme. Some of the gaps will be highlighted when you look at the management development needs identified in the various phases. For example, management development for heads of department may be perceived as a major need in the secondary sector, yet little training or support may be available in the LEA programme. You may find that some existing training courses are duplicating activities unnecessarily. For instance, one LEA found that courses for school TVEI co-ordinators, appraisers and deputy headteachers all included components on interviewing skills and report-writing, something that would not have been a problem had they not also had a common clientele. Alternatively, existing approaches to training may be inappropriate. In one LEA where management training for primary headteachers was regarded as a priority, they realized that if they continued to follow their strategy of sending heads on a 20-day management course it would take about 20 years to cover everyone. This prompted them to look for alternative strategies and activities.

The last question about the priorities for action in the short, medium and long term is probably the most difficult one to tackle. Refer back to Table 3.1 (p. 20) and check that your original assessment of the LEA's position was correct and that it is feasible for you to move forward in the way that you originally anticipated.

What you identify as a priority will depend to no small extent on the level you want to reach. For example, if you are at level 2 (many *ad hoc* courses) you may decide that reaching level 4 is a long-term priority and that in the medium term you want to

promote more training for heads and senior staff and improve course preparation and
follow-up. Of course, however desirable it may be to draw up a neat, rational list of
priorities, it is often impossible to do this. Your plan is likely to be much more
provisional and, while it is important to have a vision of what you want to achieve and
to work out a strategy for reaching it, this should not prevent you supporting worth-
while initiatives that are going on anyway. Where individuals are working with energy
and enthusiasm on some aspect of management development then it would be sensible
to support them. For example, a particular school might set up an excellent management development programme on its own, even though other schools and indeed the
LEA are only at level 1 or 2; a group of primary deputy heads might start working on
their own management development even though the LEA has made no provision for
management development for primary headteachers, let alone deputies. Enthusiasm is
all important and, when specific initiatives like this are successful, they often spill over
into other areas (e.g. primary headteachers begin to ask for management training). No
plan should be so rigid that it doesn't allow for organic growth.

Step 6: What are the Priorities for Future Work and how are we going to Achieve Systematic Management Development?

Once you have completed all the stages in the initial review, the final task is to pull
everything together, review what has been decided and check that everyone concerned
is agreed about future action. The assumption made in this chapter is that most of the
work will have been done by the co-ordinator with a small group of colleagues, and we
recognize that there may well be significant others (e.g. the CEO) whose agreement has
to be sought before you can move forward. The formal outcome of the initial review
should probably be a short report summarizing your conclusions and recommendations
and outlining a plan for future action.

Look again at the short-, medium- and long-term priorities that you identified and
decide upon a realistic timescale for tackling them (e.g. one, three or five years).
Remember that the ongoing programme will have to be maintained during this period
and this will demand a great deal of time and energy.

Another key question to consider is what resources are available. Money, or rather
the lack of it, may appear to be the central problem. Much will depend on whether or
not management development is generally regarded as a high priority for in-service. It
is likely that the co-ordinator and core team will have to spend a great deal of time
convincing colleagues and submitting bids for in-service funds for management training to the various agencies and sources (e.g. LEATGS/TVEI(E)/ESG). Frequently it
will be possible to do some work on management development without making a large
demand on resources (e.g. convincing subject-adviser colleagues – each of whom run
training for heads of department – that it might be useful to include a common
component on departmental management). The other resource questions are about
people and training agencies. It is likely that at the outset you will not have access to a
large group of good, credible, trainers and consultants. If this is the case, you should try
to take account of it in your total strategy. For example, a priority might be to second
some experienced headteachers on to a 'training-the-trainers' course. Your local

higher-education providers should be able to help you mount the type of training and support programmes required.

Are you likely to meet any barriers? Almost certainly, yes. The management development perspective is a new one in education and colleagues will not easily be persuaded to alter the way they work (see Example 6.4). This is especially the case where your priorities challenge existing practice. For example, you may want to recommend that inspectors/advisers concentrate on providing preparation and follow-up support for management development activities and not be involved in the delivery of training, or that the emphasis in provision is placed on open-learning packages teachers follow at their own time and pace. It will inevitably take many years to implement a systematic management development policy and programme and it is important to keep colleagues informed about what is happening and to try to involve them wherever possible.

Example 6.4   Strategies for raising awareness about management development

The core management development team in one LEA:

- tried to raise awareness of the management development issues in all aspects of their work;
- regularly made short reports on management development at meetings;
- circulated reports on management development in the LEA as widely as seemed sensible; and
- offered to run a workshop/short course for officer/adviser colleagues with the aim of clarifying exactly what the management development policy and programme did and could encompass.

Once you have identified the priority projects you want to tackle in the short and medium term, consider how you are going to manage these. First a word of caution: initiating too many priority areas at once may simply add to the problems of communication and co-ordination. A successful but limited project (e.g. designing a handbook for new headteachers) will be more satisfying than making little progress with a much broader topic. Specific targets and deadlines should help. The people who will be responsible for work on the priorities also need to be carefully selected. Good use can be made of teacher fellowships and secondments – but, of course, it pays to clarify in advance exactly what you want the person to do. For instance, if you are expecting to receive a written report, consider selecting someone who has had recent successful experience of writing (e.g. diploma dissertation completed). If the task is to organize a series of cluster groups then administrative skills and personality variables come into play. The eminent headteacher who has only two years before retirement may or may not be as good a choice as someone of lower status but with more relevant experience.

If the priority projects are to be successful then the people responsible for them will need to be well briefed, and given support and necessary resources (see Example 6.5).

The co-ordinator and core management development team could act as a monitoring support group and be prepared to act on the findings and conclusions. This monitoring role is centrally important. Unfortunately, there are numerous examples of teachers who have been given a secondment to do some research for the LEA and who return with their report complete only to find that times have changed and there is no one in a position to comment on it let alone act on the findings.

Example 6.5   Priority project teams

Priority topics can be tackled in a variety of ways. The first two examples are of LEAs who want to identify LEA-wide management development needs and produce specific policy recommendations.

- LEA 1: A small management development team was identified. The leader, a secondary headteacher, was given a year's secondment, the other five teacher members (four heads and a deputy from primary, middle and special schools) were given 40 days' secondment over the year. An LEA adviser and officer were full members of the team. The team interviewed teachers in schools about management development needs and provision, spoke to teachers who had recently attended a management training course and collected data about LEA-wide provision and needs. The report they produced at the end of the year formed the basis of the LEA management development policy.
- LEA 2: The LEA used the mechanism of a 20-day course to second a group of officers, advisers and teachers and gave them the task of producing a school management development policy for the authority and a strategy for implementing it.

The other two examples are of instances where the LEA was able to identify a more specific priority.

- LEA 3: Newly appointed deputy headteachers in primary schools were identified as a priority. An LEA adviser was given one day a week release for a term to undertake a specific review of the priority topic. She selected a team of six people and their report was completed in the term and recommendations for action passed to the LEA management development group.
- LEA 4: A primary headteacher was given a one-term secondment to investigate strategies for providing management training for primary headteachers.

The final task in the initial review is, as we suggested at the start of this section, to write a short report summarizing your findings and recommendations, circulate this to the appropriate people for comment and agreement and then finalize the report and the plan for action.

7

A SYSTEMATIC STRATEGY II:
PRIORITY PROJECTS

This chapter is divided into two parts. The first suggests how the LEA management development co-ordinator and core team can monitor and support the priority projects; the second part contains specific advice for the project team on the review, action and assessment phases.

Suggestions for the Management Development Co-ordinator and Core Team

There are three suggested steps for the co-ordinator and core team (see Checklist 7.1):

1. Plan how you will manage the priority projects.
2. Agree how you are going to resource, support and monitor each project.
3. Evaluate the outcomes of each project.

Checklist 7.1   Stage 2: priority projects – key steps and tasks for LEA co-ordinators

---

Step 1

Plan the specific priority projects.

Tasks

1. Review the number of projects that have to be initiated.
2. Draw up a broad timetable based upon provisional target dates for:

    (a) the completion of each project; and

(b) stage 3 overview.

3. Designate individual(s) or group(s) to carry out each project.
4. Draw up broad terms of reference for each project leader (and team).

Step 2

Agree how you are going to resource, support and monitor each project.

Tasks

1. Reach agreement with each project leader on the terms of reference, the timetable and appropriate evaluation procedures.
2. Try to ensure that each project leader has access to necessary resources (e.g. secretarial help).
3. Agree with each project leader how they will keep you informed about their work (e.g. through meetings and reports).
4. Ensure that each project leader is keeping to the timetable and is on target.
5. Remind each project leader to consult with those potentially affected and involved about the feasibility and acceptability of their likely recommendations.

Step 3

Evaluate the outcomes of each project.

Tasks

1. As each project finishes:

   (a) review the conclusions and outcomes with the leader;
   (b) where appropriate, collect the evaluation report; and
   (c) check that relevant people have been consulted.

2. Discuss your conclusions with the core team and if appropriate invite the project leader to attend this meeting.
3. Agree with the core team whether the project outcomes should be rejected or integrated into the ongoing programme.
4. Decide upon a strategy for implementing the recommendations for integration.

Step 1: Planning

The management development co-ordinator and team should plan this stage. We suggest you review the priority projects to be initiated and draw up an outline timetable for their completion (this will have to be regularly reviewed: new initiatives demanding action or a change in key personnel can seriously hinder progress). Consider when it

Example 7.1   Stage 2 timetable

Year 1
Spring term – Getting started and initial review phase.
Summer term – Setting up priority projects and planning ongoing programme.

Year 2

	Ongoing programme maintained	Meetings — Management development core team receive progress reports and feed into ongoing programme	Priority project 1: head begins one-term secondment to study management development needs of newly appointed primary heads	Priority project 2 management development for heads of department — Team leader begins one-term secondment	Priority project 3 (team-building)	Ongoing action-learning set – convenors of primary cluster groups
September	Ongoing programme maintained					
October		Meeting 1 (relate to LEATGS and LEA development plan)	Investigates needs			
November						2
December		Meeting 2	Completes report Submits to meeting 3	Interim report to meeting 3		
January				Other team members begin one day a week secondment		3
February		Meeting 3	Planning phase		Planning phase	
March April		Meeting 4	Action plan agreed at meeting 4	Progress report		4
May		Meeting 5	Advisers implement action phase	Report and recommendations to meeting 5	Deputy head on one-term secondment to learn skills	5
June				Plan action phase		
June/July		Meeting 6 (feed in to LEATGS plan)	Progress report to meeting 6	Plan for action to meeting 6 approved for September start	Report and recommendations to meeting 6	6

Year 3
September

would be appropriate to make an overview of what has been achieved. Finally, identify an individual(s) or group(s) to carry out each project. Where this involves seconding teachers from school, aim to allow time (e.g. up to one term) for preparation. Draw up some broad terms of reference for each project leader and team, and timetable regular meetings for the core management development team throughout the year (e.g. one every half term) so that you are meeting to review progress on a regular basis. A notional timetable might look like Example 7.1.

Of course, it will not always be possible to 'manage' the priority project closely. For instance, if a priority is to improve the managerial skills of TVEI co-ordinators, work in this area may be directed by the TVEI co-ordinator without close reference to the management development team. Experience has shown that in an organization as complex as an LEA it can be very difficult to make links between various activities and initiatives.

Step 2: Resource, Support and Monitor each Project

The management development co-ordinator should try to negotiate working procedures with the leader of each project, recording them in writing as a form of 'contract' so that the expectations of both parties are clear (see Example 7.2). The key points you will need to consider are included in step 2 at the beginning of this chapter. The agreement does not have to be too formal but it should be precise.

Example 7.2   Brief for a priority project

This extract is from an LEA letter from a management development co-ordinator to a headteacher about to go on a one-term fellowship at the local college of higher education:

Following our discussion last week, can I confirm that we agreed that the major purpose of your secondment is to investigate the management development needs of primary headteachers in the authority. At the end of the term you will submit a written report of your findings and recommendations. This report will go to the members of the LEA management development team in the first instance but we may decide to circulate it to all primary schools. Your supervisor at the college will help you to design the study and as arranged the three of us will meet to review progress after two weeks and again just after half term. If you have any queries about this, please do not hesitate to contact me.

In practice it is likely that the priority projects initiated will be very different. At the outset, they may be investigative studies like the one mentioned above but as the knowledge base increases so the projects may involve direct action (e.g. establishing action-learning sets among secondary deputy headteachers), as Example 7.3 indicates.

Whatever the project, you will need to consider how you are going to support, resource and monitor it. It is important that you remind project leaders to check out the feasibility and acceptability of their recommendations with those likely to be affected –

Example 7.3   Priority projects

- A secondary headteacher spends a term investigating the management development needs of secondary heads and deputies in the LEA.
- A team of six teachers (one on full-time secondment, the rest having approximately 40 days) identify management development needs across the LEA and produce policy recommendations.
- A group of teachers is formed into a writing party to produce a booklet on management development for distribution to all schools.
- A pilot course on management training for newly appointed primary deputy headteachers is organized and run.
- The LEA management development group participate in a team-building training programme.

good proposals may come to nothing if particular individuals feel threatened by them or resent the fact that they have not been consulted.

Step 3: Evaluate the Outcomes of each Project

You will need to assess the outcomes of each project as it finishes and decide what action to take. The way you do this will obviously vary from one project to another. For example, in the case of an investigative study of management development needs, you may need to collect further information (e.g. about possible training strategies) before moving to action, whereas if the project was to introduce action-learning sets, and it seems to have been successful and effective, then you might decide at once to make this a permanent feature of the programme. Example 7.4 gives two illustrative outcomes.

The key point to remember is that some response must be made, some action taken. Nothing is more disheartening for a project team than to discover that the report they worked hard to produce is gathering dust on someone's shelf.

Suggestions for the Project Leader and Team

There are three key phases to a priority project:

1. The review phase, when you investigate the issue in some detail and produce recommendations for action.
2. The action phase, when the recommendations are put into practice.
3. The evaluation or assessment phase when a decision is taken about whether or not the specific action or activity should be made a permanent feature of the policy or programme.

The three phases are summarized in Checklist 7.2.

Example 7.4   LEA responses to priority projects

LEA 1

The project team submitted their report which contained recommendations for an LEA-wide management development policy and programme.

The management development co-ordinator (the chief adviser) and the core team responded in two ways:

1. The report was distributed for comment to all schools in the LEA and to representative bodies as part of the normal consultative process prior to becoming LEA policy.
2. The team leader was appointed as part-time LEA management development co-ordinator as the LEA advisers and officers had become convinced this role was necessary.

LEA 2

The project team submitted their report on the management development needs of newly appointed deputy headteachers. Many of the recommendations related to the LEA-wide management development policy and were passed by the management development core team to the CEO for consideration. However, the project leader, a primary adviser, was asked to plan and run a training programme for primary deputy headteachers that was designed to meet the needs she and her team had identified.

Checklist 7.2   Stage 2: priority projects – key steps and tasks for the project leader and team

---

Step 1

Plan the review phase.

Tasks

1. Reach agreement with the co-ordinator on the terms of reference, the timetable and appropriate evaluation procedures.
2. Decide how you should start the project and what working methods should be employed.
3. Identify the people who should be involved or consulted or from whom information might be gathered.
4. Draw up a detailed timetable for the project.

Step 2

Summarize present policy/practice on the review topic.

Tasks

1. Establish, through document searches, interviews and observations, etc., what is present policy and practice on the topic.
2. Clarify, through document searches, interviews, observations, what the precise management development needs appear to be.
3. Decide upon criteria and procedures for assessing the effectiveness of present policy and practice and apply these.

Step 3

Assess and recommend.

Tasks

1. Judge the extent to which present practice is meeting identified needs.
2. Clarify what are your main conclusions at the end of the review phase.
3. Consider how identified but unmet needs might be dealt with.
4. Draw up your recommendations for action and check their feasibility and acceptability with those potentially affected and involved.
5. Finalize your conclusions and recommendations at the end of the review phase and:

   (a) present them to the LEA co-ordinator;
   (b) if appropriate, meet the core team to discuss them.

Step 4

Detailed planning of the action phase.

Tasks

1. Check with the co-ordinator on the terms of reference, the timetable and appropriate evaluation procedures.
2. Decide how you should start the action phase and what working methods should be employed.
3. Identify the people who should be involved or consulted or from whom information might be gathered.
4. Consider whether those involved will themselves require any in-service training and, if so, how it might be provided.
5. Draw up a detailed timetable for the action phase.

Step 5

Move into action.

Tasks

1. Implement the action.
2. Monitor the action.

Step 6

Assess the effectiveness of the action phase.

Tasks

1. Review the evaluation findings.
2. Judge the extent to which the action phase met its original aims.
3. Draft your main conclusions and recommendations.
4. Check their feasibility and acceptability with those potentially affected and involved.
5. Finalize your conclusions and recommendations at the end of the action phase and
    (a) present them to the LEA co-ordinator; and
    (b) if appropriate, meet the core team to discuss them.

Step 1: Plan the Review Phase

This will obviously be more complex if you are working with a small team rather than on your own. Nevertheless, the questions you should ask yourself remain the same. These are as follows:

1. Am I/are we clear about the terms of reference? Make sure that the management development co-ordinator and yourself are clear about what you are intending to do and about the timetable that you will be following. You may well have to review your agreement as the project gets underway; it is hard to achieve complete clarity at the outset.

    One danger is that you are over ambitious and embark on a project that you cannot possibly complete in the time available. A term can pass very quickly and experience has shown that it can take several weeks for a practising teacher or adviser to adjust to being a 'researcher' – yet this is what will probably be demanded. If you are attached to a higher-education college your supervisor should be able to advise you. Consider also what would be an appropriate way to evaluate your project.

2. How am I/are we going to conduct this project? How are you going to investigate the question that has been set? For instance, if the priority is to investigate the management development needs of secondary heads of department, how will you do

this? Questionnaire? Interviews? Seek the opinion of all heads of department or only a sample? Will you seek the views of significant others, for example, LEA advisers, headteachers? If yes, how? Will you conduct a literature search?

3. Who should be involved or consulted? Make a list of the people who should be consulted and/or involved in the process. If you are able to select your own project team, decide who should be invited to join it. Factors to consider are the credibility of the individuals and the skills they can bring to the group. If we follow through the example of the study of the management development needs of heads of department we can list these possible criteria for team members:

- Experienced and newly appointed heads of department.
- Heads of large (e.g. maths) and small (e.g. music) departments.
- Heads of science departments and heads of department in the arts/humanities area.
- Men and women.
- Headteacher and/or advisers.
- Individuals with research and writing skills.
- Individuals who are credible with colleagues and the professional associations.

The optimum size of a team is probably five or six people so you should not feel that you have to match all the criteria. Nevertheless, it will help in the long term if the project team are seen to be a fairly representative group.

As well as using your own judgement, take advice about whom it would be helpful to consult. It would obviously be sensible to seek the opinion of those subject advisers who run courses for secondary heads of department, but if you ask around you might also hear of some work being done in another LEA it would be worth following up. The final planning task is to draw up a timetable and work out exactly how you are going to fit everything in.

Step 2: Summarize Present Policy/Practice on the Review Topic

People frequently feel that the reason the topic was selected as a priority was that 'nothing was happening'. The temptation is to spend a great deal of time visiting other schools and LEAs to collect ideas, yet this can often be counterproductive. Invariably there is something valuable already happening in the LEA and it is usually much more productive to identify this and build on it rather than import practices and activities that are completely new. The techniques you use to establish present policy and practice will vary depending on the topic. Look through LEA policy papers, INSET programmes, telephone key people, etc., to establish what is happening. Even when there is no formal policy statement an implicit policy will emerge through a study of practice. Example 7.5 summarizes management development for secondary headteachers in one LEA in 1983. At this time the LEA had not yet drawn up a formal policy and programme for management development, yet there was a great deal happening none the less. Similarly, if your priority is to build up a databank of information on staff, it is most unlikely that you will find yourself starting from a position where no data are kept.

*Example 7.5   A situational analysis of management development for
              secondary headteachers*

Stage of headship	Personnel involved	Activity
Induction LEA support	Professional assistant	• Pack of materials • LEA handbook • Invitation to education department to meet officers • Visit of general adviser – suggest links and available support
	Director/deputy director Chief adviser Senior officers	Residential course for newly appointed heads (two or three days)
	General adviser	• Provision of further support or help with any specific need
	Subject advisers	• Support on curriculum matters, staff appointments, etc.
	Peer contacts and groups	• Headteacher meetings • Area headteacher groups – liaison groups contact new heads

LEA support for
   development
Early years
  (one to five years)
	Professional assistant
	General adviser
	Senior adviser for tier
	Senior adviser for area
	Subject adviser
		• Continued support
		• Provision of
		   DES circulars and publications
		   LEA circulars and digests
		• Written statements of subject/curricular initiatives and developments
		• Copies of new legislation – national and LEA policy changes

	Director and senior officers	• Annual meeting half day for secondary heads
	Director and chief adviser Senior officers and advisers	• Annual residential course for headteachers – two or three days
	Advisory division	• Course for headteachers on specific issues – two or three days residential
	Department	• Meetings to disseminate information – full day/half day

	Peer group and invited contributors	• SHA/NAHT meetings – local – termly half day Regional – termly full day • LEA headteachers' association – termly one day • Area groups – inter-tier, liaison groups. Luncheon groups, etc. termly half day
	DES	• COSMOS course. Other regional/national courses
LEA development for heads established for five years	Officers and advisory division	• Helping in LEA INSET programmes planning team, speaking, chairing groups, etc. • Representing LEA on local, regional and national bodies • Representing LEA at local, regional, national and international meetings, conference
Opportunities for self-development (any stage) usually with LEA support	Self/LEA	• Involvement in peer group/ headteacher organizations and officials, representatives on bodies, committees – attending conference – local, regional, national
	Self/LEA	• Involvement in external activities, i.e. links with industry, commerce, public services, armed forces
	Self/LEA	• Extension of personal education. Secondments for award-bearing courses, higher degrees. Sabbaticals.
	Self/LEA	• Shorter-term secondments, attachments half term–one term for courses, activities, research to a number of local providing institutions
	Regional/local/self	• 4/84 one-term training opportunity and 20-day course participation with secondments • Helping local providers on INSET programmes
	Self	• Personal involvement on local, regional and national bodies and activities reflecting heads' own specific interests, e.g. voluntary bodies, JPs, cultural bodies

	Director/chief adviser	• Counselling, support, career advice available at any stage
Transitional pre-retirement	Director/chief adviser Officers Advisory division retired head	• Opportunities for discussion and counselling • Pre-retirement course. Annually two days
Assessment/ appraisal	Chief adviser Senior adviser General adviser *Note:*	• Consultative visits. GRIDS • Informal, individual approach • Personal knowledge and contact • No systematic method of appraisal • No formal monitoring or recording of management development activities for heads • No databank of information solely concerning headteachers • Most activities after induction are *ad hoc*

(*Source:* McIntosh, 1985.)

The next task is to clarify what the precise management development needs in this area are. Undoubtedly, some broad identification of needs will have taken place at the initial review stage but a more precise analysis will almost certainly be necessary. There is a world of difference between saying, 'secondary heads of department need management development' and saying, 'secondary heads of department are requesting training in team-building skills, time management and report-writing'. You must decide how you are going to clarify the management development needs in a particular area (e.g. document searches, interviews). Take advice about the best way to do this – remember that you can usually learn as much from a carefully selected sample as from interviewing a whole cohort. One further question is worth highlighting: how likely is it that equal opportunities needs will be identified by conventional methods?

Step 3: Assess and Recommend

Once you have established present policy and practice and have clarified what the precise management development needs are then you should be ready to assess the effectiveness of present practice. Deciding on appropriate criteria and procedures for doing this is always difficult. Possible criteria include the following:

• How effective was the activity/programme in its own terms?
• What percentage of the target group were involved?
• How closely did it relate to the school situation?

- Was there an attempt to meet the management development needs of individuals at different stages of experience (e.g. newly appointed and ten years or more in post, and in relation to gender and race)?

Applying this to Example 7.5 and without making a detailed assessment of particular events we can note the following:

- No mention of preparation or follow-up for courses.
- Many activities appear to depend on individual initiative.
- The example indicates that most activities after induction were *ad hoc*.
- No real sense of a developmental support programme.

(It is, of course, also important to note that the LEA has changed considerably since the study was carried out.)

Where you are looking at one event or activity then you can apply more precise criteria, for instance, assess the effectiveness of a course on stress management for primary headteachers by looking for changes in absence rates and applications for early retirement, and by interviewing participants some months after the course. When you are able to identify precise needs, judge whether or not these are being met.

The final stage is to make some judgement about the extent to which present practice is meeting identified needs and to draw up some recommendations for action. Your recommendations will need to be realistic and feasible on two counts: first, they will have to be acceptable to the people directly concerned and, second, they must take account of existing resources. The report and recommendations can then be presented to the LEA management development co-ordinator and core team and relevant others.

The Action Phase

The action phase of the project is probably one of the most rewarding parts and yet it is also potentially one of the most problematic. Unless the action is carefully planned it may not achieve the intended objectives. We have set out our specific suggestions in key steps and tasks 4, 5, and 6 at the start of this chapter. There are three main things to do:

- Plan the action phase.
- Implement/carry out the action.
- Assess the effectiveness of the action.

These key steps are relevant whatever the action involves (e.g. introducing generic job descriptions for deputy headteachers; organizing all the authority's primary schools into cluster groups; or identifying a small group of schools and helping them to establish their own management development policy and programme.)

Step 4: Planning

The individual(s) or group(s) who have responsibility for the action phase may or may not be the same people who were involved in the review of the specific priority project.

There are obvious advantages if they are the same people in that they will already be familiar with the findings and the recommendations for action but this will not always be possible. Where new people are involved an essential first step must be for them to clarify with the co-ordinator exactly what they are being asked to do and what are their terms of reference. Once this has been agreed the project leader and team can first plan and then start the action stage.

Points to consider are the following:

- What methods should be used?
- Who should be involved and consulted?
- Will the people involved themselves need in-service training?

Step 5: Implementation

A flexible and adaptive approach to implementation is essential. Particular actions have unintended consequences. People find that they are not quite as sure how to do something as they thought they were. Key individuals fall sick. Promised resources don't materialize. The possible complications are endless. You will need to monitor the action as it is taking place and modify your plans to take account of changing circumstances. In practice it is difficult to draw up clear plans at the outset – it is more likely that you will have broad goals and objectives you are able to refine as you observe the action.

Step 6: Judging Effectiveness

The need to consider evaluation at an early stage in the process has already been mentioned. You will need to judge what form of evaluation will be most appropriate and build this into your plans. If the activity is designed as a pilot or test run, decisions will have to be taken about whether or not to continue it. It is easy for inertia to set in and for assumptions to be made that an activity or process, which seems to be working satisfactorily, should continue without making any systematic judgement about its effectiveness.

8

A SYSTEMATIC STRATEGY III: OVERVIEW AND RE-START

This chapter is mainly intended for the management development co-ordinator and members of the core team. Clearly you will need to review your overall position on LEA-wide management development from time to time and on the basis of this decide what you are going to do next. The co-ordinator and core team should be in the best position to judge when it will be appropriate to conduct an overview and should probably take the initiative in setting it up. The timing and frequency will vary but once every year or two might be sensible. The overview meeting need not be lengthy though it will need careful preparation. Ideally it should be timed to fit into the regular LEA committee cycle so that it is possible to take action on any decisions made. For example, if the overview meeting was held in June or July it should be possible to build into the September LEATGS bid additional resources for management development if these are required.

We suggest that you will need to do the following (see Checklist 8.1):

- Plan the overview procedure.
- Review the current management development policy and programme.
- Reflect on the appropriateness of the procedure for the improvement that you have adopted.
- Decide what to do next.

Step 1: Plan the Overview

One key task is to decide what is the appropriate group to conduct the overview. It may be the CEO and senior officers and advisers or alternatively a management development advisory/steering group, if one exists. Whatever the composition of the group the management development co-ordinator should ensure that they have access to

Checklist 8.1   Stage 3: overview and re-start – key steps for
co-ordinator and core team

Step 1

Plan the overview.

Tasks

1. Agree the procedures for the overview, e.g. timetable, dates for meetings.
2. Prepare a summary report on the current state of progress of:

    (a) the ongoing programme; and
    (b) the specific priority projects.

3. Distribute this summary report before the meeting.

Step 2

Review the strengths and weaknesses of the LEA policy and programme.

Tasks

1. Decide whether the ongoing programme is now meeting your needs.
2. Decide whether the new features arising from specific priority projects that have been integrated into the programme should be maintained.
3. Decide what action, if any, to take about outstanding specific priority projects.

Step 3

Decide on the usefulness of this approach as a way of achieving systematic management development.

Tasks

1. Review the extent to which the main stages and the particular working techniques recommended in this handbook were actually used.
2. Distribute this draft report to senior officers/advisers and others and seek their agreement on the conclusions and recommendations.
3. If you are going to use this approach again (perhaps in an adapted form) decide whether:

    (a) you need to conduct another initial review; or
    (b) you can move straight on to stage 3.

sufficient information to enable them to make an informed decision about the programme. This means that a summary report on the ongoing programme and any specific priority projects should be prepared and distributed before the meeting. This would not be the time to consider detailed reports on each priority area – rather a short summary of what happened and what conclusions were reached.

Step 2: Review the Strengths and Weaknesses of the LEA Policy and Programme

The central task is to decide whether the ongoing programme is now meeting LEA-wide management development needs. One way of checking this is to refer back to the original aims that were drawn up at the outset of the programme. Look again at Table 3.1 (p. 20). What level did you hope to have reached by now? Have you achieved this? Have changes occurred in the meantime that highlight new demands for management development and training? If particular strategies or activities have been introduced arising from a specific priority project, decide if they should be maintained. For example, if headteachers have been seconded to produce management training materials, consider how useful these materials have been, whether they will need to be adapted for future use and whether sufficient materials have now been prepared. Similarly, if the LEA has been organizing development activities specifically for women in middle mangement, has this had any impact on the number of women applying for and gaining senior positions in schools? If priority projects have been started but not yet completed, decide what you might do about this. For example, teachers on a one-term secondment not infrequently do not have time to complete writing up a report before they return to their schools. Without active follow-up and encouragement these reports might never be written.

Step 3: Reflect on the Appropriateness of the Procedure you have Adopted

How are you attempting to establish a more systematic management development policy and programme? If you are following the incremental approach outlined in this book, consider first how closely you have followed the suggested procedure and then reflect on the advantages and disadvantages of the approach.

If you are broadly trying to follow the procedure you may nevertheless find that, for example:

- you did not clearly designate one person as management development co-ordinator but left these tasks to a group of people;
- a core LEA management development team was not identified;
- the management development co-ordinator did not have sufficient resources (e.g. time, secretarial support) to do the job.
- a major LEA innovation, changes in key personnel or a period of teacher action wreaked havoc with your planning; or
- other significant groups in the LEA were not adequately consulted.

However, this is to be pessimistic – you may find that the strategy worked perfectly and that you have now achieved your original objectives. If the strategy worked well but you still feel there is work to be done, decide whether or not to continue with the same approach.

Step 4: Decide what to do Next

The management development co-ordinator could usefully produce a report on the overview and the conclusions that were reached as a result of this. If it is clear that work still needs to be done and the same approach is recommended, the co-ordinator should first seek any necessary agreement and resources to continue the work. Finally, decide whether another initial review is needed or if it is possible to move straight into priority projects. Unless there are radical changes in the LEA you will probably only need to conduct an initial review every two or three years.

9

A SYSTEMATIC STRATEGY IV: CASE STUDIES

Case Study 1: Management Development for Newly Appointed Primary Deputy Headteachers

This case study is based on reports written by the project leader and her colleagues. The work described took place in an authority that was following the NDC's suggested strategy for strengthening the management development programme. Senior officers in the LEA had identified a core management development team and asked them to clarify some broad policy goals, review current provision and needs, and identify areas for development. Newly appointed primary deputy headteachers were identified as a priority group and this case study outlines the steps taken to identify and meet their needs over a three-to-four-year period.

A primary adviser was asked to be the project leader and to review needs and recommend what action was required (stage 3 in the NDC development strategy). She was given a one-day-a-week secondment for a term to complete the task. The main objective was to identify the precise management needs of deputy headteachers newly appointed to primary schools from September 1985. Subsidiary tasks included an examination of management training currently afforded by the schools and the LEA, and an assessment of the suitability of this provision. Eight other people were asked to join the project team: six of them were employed as primary heads or deputies in the authority, one was a lecturer from the local polytechnic; the eighth, a retired primary head, acted as clerk to the group. They met on five occasions during the term.

They began by investigating the current position and discovered, somewhat to their surprise, that over two-thirds of the 32 new appointments made since September in that year were temporary. Some of these resulted from secondments, others because of the long-term illness of permanent post-holders or because of delays in the selection and appointment procedure (see Table 9.1).

Acting deputy headteachers within the schools came chiefly from the 45–55 age-groupings followed by slightly fewer from the 25-to-under-35 band. Very few

Table 9.1   Current position of primary staff

Types of school[1]	Male			Female			Totals
	Perm.	Acting[2]	Temp.[3]	Perm.	Acting[2]	Temp.[3]	
5–7 years			1	1	1	2	5
5–9 years		1		6	5	3	15
5–11 years	1	3	1	2	2		9
7–11 years		1			2		3
Totals	1	5	2	9	10	5	32

Notes
1. Five to eight schools had no new appointments.
2. Acting posts were internal promotions.
3. Temporary includes permanent supply staff and exchange posts.

temporary promotions came from the middle range (over 35 to under 45), which did not suggest that headteachers viewed these posts as training opportunities for permanent positions. New permanent posts ranged from over 30 to under 45, with very few within the 35-45 category. This had implications for future promotion trends. The oldest age-span applied to permanent support staff in acting deputy positions who, although their numbers were small, featured in the over-40-to-under-55 classifications only.

The next stage was to identify the management development needs of newly appointed deputy headteachers. The methods used by the project team included questionnaires, interviews, discussions, literature searches, etc. They held a group interview with 27 from their sample of 32 and this proved a very valuable source of data. The conclusions they drew from the data were these. Management development for primary-school deputy headteachers should start at the commencement of a teaching career and gather momentum when the teacher gained a responsibility allowance. Thus the appointment of a deputy head should be made in the knowledge that he or she had encountered a systematic build-up of management skills, training and experiences. The group felt this process could be divided into two stages.

Stage 1: Prior to Appointment as a Deputy Headteacher

After several years of teaching at main professional grade, all teachers should have had considerable management training in the majority of the following areas:

Professional skills

- Class-teaching experience across a wide range of age-groups preferably in more than one school.
- Working to a job description and analysing and reporting progress.
- Working alongside other colleagues, students and ancillaries.
- Assessing pupils' progress and following record-keeping procedures.
- Curriculum leadership in at least two curricular areas.
- Formulating and evaluating schemes of work.
- Developing school-focused in-service.

- Evaluating children's learning in a colleague's classroom and vice versa.
- Relating to parents individually and as a group.
- Planning, implementing and co-ordinating a school event, for example, sports' day, concert or school play.
- Taking an assembly.
- Being involved in the overall maintenance of school discipline.

Personal skills

- Leadership of discussions and contributing to discussions.
- Negotiating.
- Delegating.
- Planning as a member of a group.
- Decision-making and involvement in related processes, for example, consultation.

Administrative skills

- Report-writing.
- Minute-taking.
- Requisitioning and checking of stock.
- Statementing procedures.
- Writing a formal letter and making telephone calls on behalf of the school, for example, planning a school trip.
- Keeping accounts.

Knowledge of external agencies/people

- Understanding of teacher education in colleges, polytechnics and universities.
- Promoting links with the community and liasing with other local schools.
- Making contact with the teachers' centres.
- Developing an understanding of the LEA structure and personnel, for example, psychological service, advisory division.

Stage 2: From being a Deputy Headteacher Designate until Approximately Two Years of Service has Elapsed in that Post

Management development and training at this stage should take full account of the opportunities presented to the appointee in previous years. Gaps and weaknesses should be identified and remedied and strengths should not be allowed to dissipate. This is the period during which interpersonal skills, knowledge of school and LEA personnel, decision-making, communication skills and administrative expertise should be fostered rapidly. Much can be done in the two-month period prior to the appointment taking effect and, although the following list does not purport to be exhaustive, the deputy should become informed about and/or involved in the following important areas at this stage:

The school organization and its procedures

- Staffing, allocation of responsibility posts, job descriptions.
- Timetabling, devising rotas.
- Staff meetings and internal communication systems.
- Staff absenteeism and supply cover.
- Pupil admission policies.
- Emergency and safety procedures, for example, accidents, first-aid, hospital, police and fire.
- Duties and appointments of ancillaries, for example, NTAs, nursery nurses, secretary, school superintendent, cleaners and school-meals staff.
- School-meals arrangements.
- Security arrangements.

Counselling and interviewing   Development of the staff-tutor role would be advantageous. If this post is allocated already, there will be other opportunties available to the newly appointed deputy headteacher, for example, assisting with the induction of new colleagues. Counselling skills are regarded as particularly important:

- Observation of some interviews at main professional grade at the discretion of headteacher, chair of governors and LEA.
- Interviewing parents.
- Conducting teacher appraisals.

Curricular provision

- Knowledge of national curriculum policy documents and guidelines.
- Knowledge of particular ongoing activities, for example, LMS, GRIDS.
- Knowledge of evaluation processes.

Legislation   Becoming better informed about legislation affecting education, education Acts and equal-opportunities policies and regulations.

Outside agencies   Knowing how to contact appropriate representatives from the following:

- Welfare, school meals, caretaking, medical, psychological, social and leisure services.
- Advisory and development divisions.
- Governing body.
- Community education, neighbourhood schools and colleges.
- Police.
- PTA.

Administration

- Knowledge of a wide variety of forms and experience of completing many of them.
- Familiarity with the school filing-system.

- Documentation regarding special needs.
- Involvement in short-listing.
- Working knowledge of the school's handbook.

Further Management Development for Deputy Headteachers

The group felt that it was essential that management training should be continued and consolidated so that experienced deputies could discharge their responsibilities more effectively and would be thoroughly prepared for headship if they had the ability and motivation to apply for it.

The project team were at the same time collecting information about existing management development opportunities for primary deputy headteachers. Their findings were not especially encouraging. They learned that mangement training within schools largely relied upon the opportunities provided by the headteacher, made available by changing circumstances or sought by the teacher concerned. Not surprisingly, some teachers were seriously disadvantaged by the superficial, incomplete and fragmented staff development they encountered. Irrespective of promotional prospects, such a situation meant that teacher expertise was wasted and that job satisfaction was not fully realized. Stereotyping of curriculum leadership posts (e.g. science posts for men and language posts for women) and of class-teaching responsibilities (e.g. men were often expected to teach the oldest age-groups and women the youngest) hindered the development of a broad range of professional skills.

Overall the project team concluded that there was firm evidence of serious deficiencies in management training. Very few newly appointed deputy headteachers had job descriptions and most had no specific understanding of administration, finance, evaluation and legal considerations. In addition, a sizeable group had no experience of timetabling or of the assessment of students and probationers.

In-service training was available in the LEA for primary deputy headteachers. It ranged from the long award-bearing courses (e.g. in-service B Ed and diploma in primary education) to one-term secondments and some shorter management training courses. However, the project team felt that such in-service education frequently attempted to cover an extensive range of aspects (of which management was but one), was open to applications from 'any primary-school teacher' or attempted to match the needs of deputy headteachers of first, middle and high schools without being more precisely tailored to the type of school or experience of individual course members. There were few management courses for middle managers in primary schools. However, LEA curriculum working parties, discussion groups, planning teams and meetings often provided considerable assistance in management training. Also LEA advisers and support staff took an active part in staff development and promoted whole-school management training.

Specific recommendations for action were drawn up on the basis of the review of needs and existing provision. The project team concluded that, with few exceptions, the management needs of newly appointed primary deputy headteachers in the authority's schools had not been either recognized or met. Management training deficiencies prior to and during middle-management appointments produced a back-log, which it was virtually impossible to alleviate at a later stage. They concluded that until management development was viewed as a continuous and inter-dependent process, there would be serious gaps in training, ill-conceived deployment of human and material resources, wastage of talent and potential and a consequent depression of job satisfaction. They noted that though women teachers greatly outnumbered men in the authority's primary schools, 60 per cent of deputy headships in 5–11 schools and 70 per cent in 7–11 junior schools were held by men. This was a key issue in an LEA committed to equal opportunities. The situation was particularly disturbing when seen in the context of the full analysis of all permanent deputy headship appointments including their age-groupings and contracting career avenues. It was probable that by 1990 the majority of deputy headteachers in the authority's primary schools would be over 45 years, with many nearing retirement. This had serious implications for future headteacher appointments.

The following was recommended:

1. Management development and training in the authority's primary schools should be afforded a high priority by schools, the LEA and institutions of higher education.
2. Management development should be seen as a continuum comprising various stages such as the following:

   • Middle management.
   • Newly appointed deputy headteachers.
   • Experienced deputy headteachers.
   • Deputy headteachers of long standing.
   • Newly appointed headteachers.
   • Experienced headteachers.

3. A policy document should be formulated indicating the specific contribution which the schools, the LEA and the regional providers of in-service education may make to a comprehensive and cohesive training programme. The policy should take account of the primary-needs programme.
4. A management development course specifically for primary deputy headteachers should be organized.
5. Particular attention should be given to the differing management needs of acting deputy headteachers from within the school and to those appointed as permanent supply staff.
6. Special consideration should be given to the value of teacher exchange (for one year minimum) at middle-management level and to regular meetings of deputy headteachers, for example, through a professional association.
7. Urgent attention should be given to full analysis of all deputy headteacher appointments each term so that it was possible:

   (a) to identify trends, especially in view of new governing body arrangements; and
   (b) to make predictions about staffing at deputy headship and headship levels.

The recommendation that a management course should be run for primary deputy headteachers was agreed quickly, and the primary adviser (who had acted as project leader) designed and led what became a series of courses. Preference was given to newly appointed deputy headteachers when participants were selected. The course design emphasized practical, problem-solving activities that focused on specific management skills. Group discussions formed a major element. From the information obtained from participants in advance, it was evident that some deputies had had no experience of chairing a group discussion. Surprisingly, not all had even contributed to group discussions (other than an informal 'chat' in the staffroom), and only a minority had been asked to represent a group by disseminating their viewpoints publicly to a sizeable audience. Each group discussion was monitored by an advisory teacher who did not engage in the discussion but observed what was happening and provided feedback about process points at the end of the session. Participants were given specific training in handling group discussions and with regular practice with feedback, there was a marked improvement in their performance.

This attention to process issues was a marked feature of the course. Participants tackled practical tasks concerned with school-staffing allocations, reference-writing, and the management of school meals, but attention was also paid to their interpersonal and communication skills and their ability to work as a member of a team.

The course leader argued that management training courses need to identify weaknesses (as well as strengths), to provide strategies for dealing with and eradicating skill deficiencies and to build up systematically the range and depth of expectations so that the manager has both confidence and sensitivity. She concluded that a number of distinct characteristics of management training courses had emerged as significant. Seeking basic information about participants' needs in advance and allowing the courses to be structured upon these findings and other subsequent assessments of the position meant that the courses could be pitched with some confidence at a level appropriate to the members' needs. Although planned in outline well in advance, she felt the training should be dynamic and reflect the responses received during each week's sessions. Equally, they must take account of the assignments and their outcomes. Such courses demand extreme hard work from the course leader as, if they are devised simply as a presentation of pre-planned packages (all probably used several times previously with different groups), they will demonstate their own irrelevance, appear sterile and lack inspiration. At their best they should epitomize a joint learning process by the leader and the members bounded by a knowledge that they are working to some common and essential purpose.

Case Study 2: Management Development for Primary Headteachers

Introduction and Background

In 1984, the LEA ran its first 20-day management course for primary headteachers. This course was repeated in 1985–6 by which time some 30 headteachers had been trained. The course director was the senior secondary adviser assisted by one of his primary-adviser colleagues. Though the course was well received by participants, the director felt that it could be improved and also became concerned that only a small number of headteachers could take part in it. He estimated that since there were approximately 156 primary schools in the county it would take 20 years to train each head and deputy using the 20-day primary management course as a vehicle. This was also discounting the management development needs of other senior staff (e.g. curriculum post-holders).

Faced with this problem, he decided that the LEA needed more information about how other LEAs were providing management development for primary headteachers and, accordingly, in 1986 he seconded a headteacher to undertake a one-term investigative study. The brief for this headteacher was that she should examine a number of 20-day primary management courses and make recommendations 'for change/consolidation' in the course.

Study and Report

During her one-term secondment the headteacher visited a number of primary management courses and one LEA, which had adopted a particular approach to training. She also conducted a questionnaire survey of primary heads and deputies and a survey of those who had completed the 20-day course in order to ascertain their views on management training. Key factors highlighted in her report were:

- that experienced headteachers were frequently used as trainers in other LEAs;
- that it was important to provide follow-up for management courses;
- that one LEA had organized a group of headteachers and advisers to develop a training programme for each area of the authority; and
- that primary heads and deputies were anxious to receive management training and felt that it should be given a high priority.

The report contained a number of recommendations for action by the LEA. For example:

- that two primary 20-day courses should be run each year;
- that deputies as well as headteachers should be selected as participants;
- that a group of headteachers should be selected to form a primary-advisory group who would work with the primary adviser and course director to discuss how they might make an input to the course; and
- that primary schools should be organized into professional support groups for management training purposes.

The completed report was passed to the LEA management development co-ordinator for consideration. He discussed with officer and adviser colleagues how the LEA might respond.

Responses

The LEA decided to implement many of the specific recommendations. In particular it established a primary management advisory group that consisted of a small group of headteachers, the primary adviser and course director, and it decided to set up primary professional support groups. In September 1986 all primary schools were grouped into a cluster based on their local comprehensive school. Each cluster elected one person as convenor and he or she became a member of one of four area steering committees. It was made clear that the cluster groups were expected to meet twice a term. These meetings would be:

1. a management training session involving 'self-help' packs
2. a meeting for professional exchange when useful solutions and suggestions for tackling school problems can be discussed and fed back to area steering groups.

The primary management advisory group would advise the LEA on the planning and co-ordination of this initiative.

The primary headteacher who had conducted the review was given a further one-term secondment to help set up the cluster groups and the area steering committees. A second headteacher was given a one-term secondment with the brief to develop a pack of management training materials for use in the cluster groups.

The cluster groups and area steering committees were set up and received a very positive response from the headteachers (over 90 per cent of them attended one of the four initial meetings – one in each area). Convenors were elected and 100 per cent of convenors attended the subsequent area steering group meeting and planned activities for the following term. A self-help pack of training materials was developed and trialled. In all, the initiative appeared to have begun well, although it was too early to make a complete evaluation. There were several unintended consequences:

- Staff in one local college of education heard about the cluster system and offered their help in providing management training either on courses or with cluster groups.
- Other groups in the LEA (e.g. reading teacher advisers) became interested in the cluster system and began to explore how they could use it for their own work.
- The LEA management development co-ordinator and his adviser/officer colleagues realized that though the cluster system had originally been set up to provide management training and support for headteachers, it could be used for general staff-development purposes and to service the new INSET programmes after April 1987.
- The authority aimed to give ownership of the scheme to the schools through the primary management advisory group. Much of the third primary course of 1986–7 was tutored by headteachers who had attended previous county courses. A similar group of heads was commissioned to develop a training programme for deputies. This was most successful and was being repeated.

Conclusions

This short case study illustrates clearly several points:

1. The need for a responsive, flexible approach to planning (at the start of the review stage the LEA had no intention of setting up a cluster group system).
2. Everyone involved gained a clearer notion of the scope of the priority project while it was taking place. The initial purpose, which was to see how a 20-day primary management course could be improved, was changed into a proposal that would enable all the LEA's primary heads to have access to some form of management training.

3. The LEA management development co-ordinator played a crucial role throughout – arranging the initial secondment; ensuring that the proposals in the review report were considered and discussed; implementing the recommendations that were agreed; and arranging two further secondments to try to ensure that the cluster system was introduced successfully.

4. The LEA management development co-ordinator must monitor the priority projects on an ongoing basis; an individual headteacher can do little without LEA guidance and support.

5. This seems to have been a very effective use of one-term fellowships. The fellows produced information and materials when they were required and their work formed part of a clear LEA strategy.

Case Study 3: Preparing an LEA Management Development Policy

This case study is based on the experience of working as consultant with an LEA as it drew up a management development policy for the authority.

Background

The work described here took place in a large rural county that had 33 secondary schools and 253 primary schools. The LEA had a well-established pattern of management training provision for primary and secondary headteachers and senior staff. A key element was a 20-day management training course for secondary heads and deputies, which had run for a number of years. Indeed, the experience of this course led indirectly to the desire to establish a management development policy. By 1986–7, all the secondary headteachers and several deputies had received management training, as had several primary headteachers. A number of these senior teachers began to raise questions with LEA officers and advisers about what might happen next, what provision was available for other teachers (e.g. middle managers) and how management training fitted with other aspects of LEA policy. This prompted the LEA to consider what would be the best way of framing such a policy.

Initial Planning

The CEO and his senior colleagues decided to engage a consultant to work with a group of LEA officers, advisers, headteachers and teachers on the task of producing an LEA-wide school management development policy. Several preliminary meetings were held between the consultant and a group of officers and advisers to discuss what was the best way to work and who might be involved in the policy-making group. The LEA had already decided that administratively the exercise should be handled like a 20-day management course. About 24 people were invited to join the group. Participants were drawn from the team of LEA officers and advisers, primary, secondary, special and further-education sectors. Care was taken to ensure that the group included deputies and middle managers as well as headteachers, women as well as men, and the chief adviser was also a member. A secondary deputy headteacher was seconded to co-ordinate the whole exercise. Twenty days were allocated for the work over the year and the co-ordinator was seconded for two days a week.

Aim

The purpose of the exercise was to produce a school management development policy for the authority and to make recommendations about how the policy might be implemented.

Working Methods

A half-day meeting was held to launch the exercise and to enable people to meet each other. Following this the time was roughly divided between meetings, usually two-day residentials, when the group met to discuss their ideas and recommendations, and days when they met in phase groups for visits, reading, etc.

The NDC suggestions about how to develop a strategic management development policy were used as a structuring device for the work. The first activity was a three-day residential meeting during which participants checked out their understanding of management development, and reviewed the provision of management training, education and support for teachers in all types of school across the authority. Following this, participants worked in phase groups, to establish what they felt the management development needs were and how these might be met. Information was gathered in a variety of ways, for example, interviews with headteachers and teachers, visits to schools known to provide good school-based management training and support, visits to personnel officers in local industrial firms and relevant reading. The phase groups then brought their ideas and suggestions back and shared them with the others at a meeting of the plenary group. The co-ordinator handled all the administrative work (e.g. booking venues for meetings, arranging for reports and papers to be typed and distributed, etc.). The programme of work and activities was planned by the consultant and co-ordinator in consultation with a small steering committee, which consisted of one person from each of the phase groups.

Finally, at the end of the year, after a great deal of hard work and much heated discussion, the group had produced a draft management development policy that the CEO was prepared to support, and some recommendations about how the policy might be implemented. They had also written some exemplar and training materials for heads and teachers in primary and secondary schools.

Next Steps

The draft policy document was sent out for consultation across the authority and was adopted as LEA policy in the next school year. A small management development steering committee, which included several of the original group, was established and a dissemination strategy was agreed. Headteachers and teachers were informed about the management development policy in a variety of ways, for example, at headteacher meetings, through discussions on school in-service training days, by receiving copies of the documentation and by an LEA-produced video on management development that was made available to schools. The policy formed a framework for planning subsequent management development activities in the authority.

Looked at objectively it could be said that this was a rather lengthy and expensive way of drawing up a management development policy. However, the strategy the LEA chose to follow did have some distinct benefits. First, and probably most important, the policy that emerged was supported by key personnel from all phases of the authority including further-education advisers and officers as well as heads and teachers. Second, the 20-day programme of work was a staff-development activity for the participants, several of whom had opportunities to develop and practice new skills (e.g. producing reports and training materials). Third, participants from different phases did find that they faced similar problems. It was the first time the LEA had brought together the further-education, special, primary and secondary phases and though there were many different perspectives, the group members found that they could agree on common policy objectives. Participants did learn from each other, as the organizers had hoped, and they did gain a clearer understanding of what was happening across the whole authority.

The exercise did help to highlight the equal-opportunities issue in the authority. As in many LEAs, women were proportionally under-represented in senior-management positions, so the women participants, especially those from secondary schools, were deputies and heads of department rather than headteachers. Many of the male head-teachers were unused to engaging in dialogue with 'junior' women colleagues about management questions, and this added an interesting dimension to group discussions.

10

CONCLUSIONS: SCHOOL MANAGEMENT DEVELOPMENT AS AN INNOVATION

This handbook contains ideas for strengthening school management development by moving towards a more coherent, policy-led scheme. We have suggested that an incremental approach should be adopted in which broad goals are identified at the outset (e.g. level 4 on Table 3.1 – p. 20), and a strategy for achieving these goals over a number of years is worked out. We recognize that this is a difficult task that cannot be achieved quickly. In turn, LEAs will also recognize that the implementation of systematic management development requires a long period of time (a minimum of five years) to develop the necessary knowledge and skills, the professional infrastructure, the shared experience, understanding and professional vocabulary, the attitudes and the overall culture that will be important pre-conditions and features of a systematic management development scheme. According to Everard (1986), it took ICI twenty years to create the culture needed for a successful management development strategy, so even five years may well be an optimistic estimate for larger LEAs.

Enough is now known about effective change strategies for us to suggest, with some confidence, ways in which CEOs and their senior colleagues should approach this task. First, due account must be taken of the characteristics of the innovation itself, in this case school management development. Undoubtedly, many of the procedures and activities of management development are familiar to LEAs, but the concept of management development as a coherent, policy-led strategy for maximizing the use of human (professional) resources to improve teaching and learning is much less familiar. Many LEA staff find it difficult to grasp the nature and scope of management development. In particular they have difficulty in making connections between management development and other aspects of the LEA's work. Systematic management development schemes require LEAs to integrate and co-ordinate action on a wide variety of fronts. Many of these aspects of LEA policy are at an early stage of development and in any case have been complicated by the Education Reform Act and associated developments. It is therefore not surprising that within this dynamic and changing context, LEAs find it difficult to connect them all together into a coherent policy.

Next, account must be taken of the characteristics of the LEAs themselves. Following the Education Reform Act there will be 116 LEAs in England and Wales, all of which vary considerably in their capacity and readiness to adopt systematic management development. Research tells us that the crucial factors affecting the fate of innovations relate to the settings in which they are to be introduced. Relatively little research has been done on the characteristics of LEAs, so what follows are simply our reflections on experience. Although it may seem trite to emphasize that each LEA is unique, it is nevertheless true and important. Each LEA's procedures for INSET and management development all have a bearing on the introduction of systematic management development. One major barrier to the introduction of systematic management development across an LEA lies in the structure of LEAs themselves. LEAs, especially larger ones, have organizational structures (e.g. area divisions) and differentiation of roles for advisers and officers (e.g. area, age phase and subject) that together make it difficult to implement LEA-wide policies. Area, subject and phase advisers often operate semi-independently of each other on, for instance, the criteria for selecting course participants as well as on different aspects of LEA policy, such as the introduction of TVEE, and this may well be affected or complicated by recent moves towards re-structuring.

The importance of structural variations can be illustrated with several examples. First, a small urban LEA with a centrally based team of advisers poses tasks and problems that require different solutions from those of a large county LEA with a devolved divisional structure. Second, an LEA in which elected members play an active interventionist role in the implementation as well as the formulation of policy is quite different from an authority in which this is not the case. Third, the LEA that has devolved control of a substantial proportion of the LEATGS budget to schools requires a different approach to management development from the LEA that retains a largely centralized system. Fourth, LEAs that already have mechanisms for integrating major policy initiatives such as TVEE and appraisal into their overall training schemes, will be in a much stronger position to integrate them with a management development policy than those that do not.

Several additional features of LEAs also act as barriers. For example, LEAs themselves rarely have a personnel function and local-authority personnel officers are normally involved to only a limited degree in the work of LEAs with teachers and heads. Similarly, most LEAs do not have an adequate or accessible data-base on the teachers and headteachers in their schools and, in consequence, they are not in a position to make informed decisions about, for instance, the likely rate of headteacher retirement in primary schools over the next five years and the consequent induction of new heads.

Nevertheless, though there are undoubtedly barriers to easy implementation of management development, it is also important to note that the NDC has not encountered any significant resistance to the idea of management development from LEAs. In general LEAs have been receptive to the ideas in this handbook when they have engaged with them at conferences, individual meetings and during consultancies. A

1988 NDC survey (Wallace and Hall) revealed that 30 per cent of LEAs already had or were in the course of developing a written management development policy, while more than half said that they were now adopting a more systematic approach to management development. We therefore conclude that the barriers to the introduction of systematic management development in LEAs can be overcome.

Finally, account must be taken of the characteristics of the central management team and their change strategy. LEAs will recognize that to ensure the implementation of a scheme of such fundamental and strategic importance, they will need to commit a substantial proportion of the time of senior officers and advisers over a lengthy period. Too often senior staff devote the necessary time to an innovation at the outset but are very quickly pulled away to carry out other duties. Although this is understandable it should obviously be avoided where possible, especially in this case because – if properly implemented – school management development is a strategic mechanism for ensuring that the multiple changes resulting from the Education Reform Act are effectively implemented.

In summary, therefore, our main suggestions for LEAs are as follows:

- Recognize that systematic school management development is a complex innovation that will take five to ten years to put into place, depending on the starting-point.
- Ensure that management development contributes to other initiatives within the framework of the LEA's overall development plan.
- Make management development policy and funding an integral part of the overall INSET strategy.
- Support schools in improving their own school-level management development schemes.
- The management training required to implement the Education Reform Act and related developments such as appraisal and TVEE should be centrally supported and co-ordinated to ensure coherence and consistency and to avoid duplication.

BIBLIOGRAPHY AND REFERENCES

Adair, J. (1979) *Action Centred Leadership*, Gower, Aldershot.

Adair, J. (1984) *The Skills of Leadership*, Gower, Aldershot.

Bank, J. (1985) *Outdoor Development for Managers*, Gower, Aldershot.

Barnett, B. (1985) Peer-assisted leadership: using research to improve practice, *The Urban Review*, Vol. 17, no. 1, pp. 47–64.

Barnett, B. *et al.* (1984a) *Elementary Principals' Yellow Pages*, Far West Laboratory for Educational Research and Development, San Francisco, Calif.

Barnett, B. *et al.* (1984b) *Secondary Principals' Yellow Pages*, Far West Laboratory for Educational Research and Development, San Francisco, Calif.

Beck, T. and Kelly, M. (1989) Using consultancy to help train managers in education, *British Journal of Inservice Education*, Vol. 15, no. 1, pp. 19–24.

Beeby, J.M. and Rathborn, S. (1983) Development training – using the outdoors in management development, *Management Education and Development*, Vol. 14, no. 3, pp. 170–81.

Belbin, R.N. (1981) *Management Teams: Why They Succeed or Fail*, Heinemann, London.

Boydell, T. (1973) *A Guide to Job Analysis*, BACIE, London.

Boydell, T. and Pedlar, M. (1978) *A Manager's Guide to Self-Development*, Gower, Aldershot.

Cooper, C.L. (ed.) (1981) *Improving Interpersonal Relations*, Gower, Aldershot.

Day, C. *et al.* (1985) *Managing Primary Schools: A Professional Development Approach*, Paul Chapman, London.

Department of Education and Science (1989) *Second Letter to CEOs on Appraisal*, DES, London.

Dunham, J. (1984) *Stress in Teaching*, Croom Helm, London.

Elliott, J. (1978) What is action research in schools?, *Journal of Curriculum Studies*, Vol. 10, no. 4, pp. 53, 58.

Elliott, J. (1980) Implications of classroom research for professional development, in E. Hoyle and J. Megarry (eds.) *World Yearbook of Education 1980: Professional Development of Teachers*, Kogan Page, London.

Everard, B. (1986) *Developing Management in Schools*, Blackwell, Oxford.

Francis, D. and Woodcock, M. (1982) *50 Activities for Self-Development*, Gower, Aldershot.

Goulding, S. *et al.* (eds.) (1984) *Case Studies in Educational Management*, Paul Chapman, London.

Gray, H.L. (ed.) (1982) *The Management of Educational Institutions*, Falmer, Lewes.

Hall, V. and Oldroyd, D. (1989) *Management Self-Development*, National Development Centre for School Management Training, Bristol.

Honey, P. and Mumford, A. (1982) *The Manual of Learning Styles*, Peter Honey, Ardingley House, 10 Linden Avenue, Maidenhead, Berks. SL6 6HB.

Hopkins, D. (1985) *A Teacher's Guide to Action Research*, Open University Press, Milton Keynes.

Huczynski, A. (1983) *An Encyclopedia of Management Development Methods*, Gower, Aldershot.

Joyce, B.R. and Showers, B. (1980) Improving in-service training: the messages of research, *Educational Leadership*, February, pp. 379–85 (reprinted in Hopkins, D. (1986) *A Teacher's Guide to Action Research*, Open University Press, Milton Keynes).

Joyce, B. and Showers, B. (1988) *Student Achievement Through Staff Development*, Longman, London.

Kolb, D. (1976) *The Learning Style Inventory: Technical Manual*, McBer, Boston, Mass.

Kolb, D. and Fry, R. (1975) Toward an applied theory of experiential learning, in C.L. Cooper (ed.) *Theories of Group Processes*, Wiley, Chichester.

Kubr, M. (ed.) (1976) *Management Consulting: A Guide to the Profession*, International Labour Office, Geneva.

Lacey, J.D. and Licht, N.C. (1980) Culminating experience: a tool for management training, *Training and Development Journal*, Vol. 34, no. 3, pp. 88–90.

Langrish, S. (1981) Assertiveness training, in C. Cooper (ed.) *Improving Interpersonal Relations*, Gower, Aldershot.

Local Government Training Board (1984) *The Effective Manager: a Resource Handbook*, LGTB, Arndale House, Luton, Beds. LU1 2TS.

Lyons, G., Stenning, R. and McQueeney, J. (1986) *Managing Staff in Schools: Training Materials*, Hutchinson, London.

Mackay, I. (1980) *A Guide to Asking Questions*, BACIE, London.

Mackay, I. (1984) *A Guide to Listening*, BACIE, London.

Manpower Services Commission (1984) *Management Self-Development: A Practical Manual for Managers and Trainers*, MSC, Moorfleet, Sheffield S1 4PQ.

McIntosh, M. (1985) *Towards a Management Development Policy for Headteachers in Secondary Schools: A Study of Needs, Tasks and Resources*, National Development Centre for School Management Training, Bristol.

McMahon, A., Bolam, R., Abbott, R. and Holly, P. (1984) *Guidelines for Review and Internal Development in Schools: Primary and Secondary School Handbooks*, Longman for the Schools Council, York.

McNiff, J. (1988) *Action Research: Principles and Practice*, Macmillan Education, Basingstoke.

Megginson, D. and Boydell, T. (1979) *A Manager's Guide to Coaching*, BACIE, London.

Miles, M.B. (1959) *Learning to Work in Groups: A Program Guide for Educational Leaders*, Teachers' College, Columbia University, New York, NY.

Morgan, C., Hall, V. and Mackay, H. (1983) *The Selection of Secondary School Headteachers*, Open University Press, Milton Keynes.

Mortimore, P., Sammons, P., Stolle, L., Lewis, D. and Ecob, R. (1988) *School Matters: The Junior Years*, Open Books, Wells, Somerset.

Mumford, A. (1980) *Making Experience Pay*, McGraw-Hill, Maidenhead.

National Steering Group (1989) *Final Report on the Teacher Appraisal Pilot Schemes*, DES, London.

Paisey, A. (1984) *School Management: A Case Approach*, Paul Chapman, London.

Pedlar, M. (ed.) (1983) *Action Learning in Practice*, Gower, Aldershot.

Phipson, G. and Smith, K. (1982) Exchanging jobs, in R. Bolam (ed.) *School-Focused In-Service Training*, Heinemann, London.

Reddy, M. (1985) Counselling in organizations, *Training Officer*, Vol. 21, no, 8, pp. 236–9.

Revans, R.W. (1972) Action learning – a management development programme, *Personnel Review*, Vol. 1, no. 4, pp. 356–62.

Revans, R.W. (1984) *The Sequence of Managerial Achievement*, MCB University Press, Buckingham.

Robson, M. (ed.) (1984) *Quality Circles in Action*, Gower, Aldershot.

Rutter, M., Maughan, B., Mortimore, P. and Ouston, J. (1979) *Fifteen Thousand Hours: Secondary Schools and their Effects on Children*, Open Books, London.

Schmuck, R. and Runkel, P. (1985) *The Handbook of Organisation Development in Schools* (3rd edn), Mayfield, London.

Secondary Heads Association (1989) *If It Moves: A Study of the Role of the Deputy Head*, SHA, London.

Showers, B. (1985) Teachers coaching teachers, *Educational Leadership*, April, pp. 43–8.

Smith, R.M. (1983) *Learning how to Learn*, Open University Press, Milton Keynes.

Stuart, R. (1978) Contracting to learn, *Management Education and Development*, Vol. 7, no. 5, pp. 43–65.

Styan, D. (1989) *School Management Task Force: Interim Report* (mimeo 23pp), DES, London.

Taylor, W. (1973) *Heading for Change*, Routledge & Kegan Paul, London.

Taylor, C. (1977) Shadowing: the creative approach to supervisory training, *Management*, Vol. 24, no. 8, pp. 14–15.

Taylor, J.L. and Walford, R. (1978) *Learning and the Simulation Game*, Open University Press, Milton Keynes.

Ungerson, B. (1983) *How to Write a Job Description*, Institute of Personnel Management, London.

Wallace, M. (1986) *A Directory of School Management Development Activities and Resources*, NDCSMT, Bristol University School of Education, Bristol.

Wallace, M. (1987) A historical review of action research: some implications for the education of teachers in their managerial role, *Journal of Education for Teaching*, Vol. 13, no. 2, pp. 97–115.

Wallace, M. (1988) *Towards Effective Management Training Provision*, NDCSMT, Bristol University School of Education, Bristol.

Wallace, M. and Butterworth, B. (1987) *Management Development in Small Primary Schools*, NDCSMT, Bristol University School of Education, Bristol.

Wallace, M. and Hall, V. (1989) Management Development and Training for Schools in England and Wales: An Overview. *Educational Management and Administration*, Vol. 17, no. 4, p. 163–76.

Woodcock, M. (1979) *Team Development Manual*, Gower, Aldershot.

Woodcock, M. and Francis, D. (1979) *The Unblocked Manager: A Practical Guide to Self-Development*, Gower, Aldershot.

Woodcock, M. and Francis, D. (1981) *Organisation Development Through Teambuilding*, Gower, Aldershot.

INDEX